WALKING IN
THE YORKSHIRE DALES

Colin Speakman is a lifelong rambler. Having worked as a Lecturer in English, a Principal Assistant with the Yorkshire National Park Department, and a Project Officer with the Countryside Commission, he now works full time as a writer and consultant, living close to the edge of Ilkley Moor, where "the real Dales country begins".

For many years he has been an active member of the Ramblers' Association, and is the founder-Secretary of the Yorkshire Dales Society, a Dales-based charity formed to ensure the conservation and interpretation of this unique part of England's heritage.

Also by Colin Speakman and published by Robert Hale
A Yorkshire Dales Anthology

WALKING IN
THE YORKSHIRE DALES

by

Colin Speakman

ROBERT HALE · LONDON

ISBN 0 7090 2166 6

Robert Hale Limited
Clerkenwell House
Clerkenwell Green
London EC1R 0HT

Photoset by Rowland Phototypesetting Ltd
Printed in Great Britain by
St Edmundsbury Press, Bury St Edmunds, Suffolk
Bound by Woolnough Bookbinding Ltd, Northants

Contents

Illustrations

Picture Credits

All photographs by the author except numbers 15 and 16 by Eliza Forder (Dales Photos, Dent).

Maps

All the maps are based upon the Ordnance Survey map with the permission of the Controller of Her Majesty's Stationery Office, Crown Copyright Reserved.

Acknowledgements

My thanks to members of the local farming communities in the Yorkshire Dales, who must inevitably have more people crossing their land – hopefully, as readers of this book, the more considerate kind; to the Yorkshire Dales National Park Committee, North Yorkshire County Council and Bradford District Council and their officers who so diligently keep the footpaths in repair and well signposted; to the Ramblers' Association, local Areas and Groups, who, over the decades, have helped keep our footpath network in being and ensured its use; to the compilers of the many footpath maps and field guides who have contributed to my own knowledge and understanding of the area.

And to Pauline Donald, who typed the manuscript so efficiently, to Keith Lockyer whose help with photography was invaluable, and finally to my wife who, as reader of the manuscript and compiler of the index, and in so many other significant ways, has helped turn this book into reality.

For my parents,
who first shared a love of a country footpath.

1

An Introduction

This book is a celebration – a celebration of a uniquely beautiful English landscape, the Yorkshire Dales.

I do not apologize for starting with the beauty, the sheer breathtaking exhilarating physical beauty of the landscape of the Yorkshire Dales, because that is what this book is all about.

It might be suggested – and I would not argue – that the artist, the painter and the photographer have the advantage in communicating the visual splendours of a landscape like the Dales. Words are, after all, poor approximations for visual imagery.

Yet the writer, I would argue, has a very special contribution to make. It is the writer as much as the painter who has shaped our attitude to the countryside. After all, not even a Turner, a Cotman or a Girtin can do full justice to the dazzling variety and the subtlety perceived by the human eye; and not all the recent developments of photography and television, techniques that have brought the beauty of the Dales into millions of homes, can fully capture that special quality that remains to be enjoyed at first hand.

But the writer, in however humble a way, can direct the reader's eye, sharpen his powers of perception, allow him to share an experience, at least in his mind's eye.

The only way physically to share that experience of the landscape is on foot. I do not claim that the rambler is the only person who sees and understands the beauty around him; most countrymen, especially the hill farmer, the shepherd, the gamekeeper, will, when going about their ordinary business, suddenly look up and be aware of the splendour around them. But I do claim that only if you have time to be absorbed into a landscape, to note its many quiet changes of mood and feeling, to use your other senses so betrayed by modern civilization – your sense of touch, smell, of sound, even of taste – can you begin to understand what the Dales are all about. Most of us who live in drab towns or suburbs can only escape briefly into the landscape of our dreams. Those moments are precious to us; we must enjoy them to the full.

For many people the thought of walking a dozen miles or so even in a landscape as lovely as the Yorkshire Dales appears as a kind of masochism. Why indeed walk, when you can enjoy the speed and comfort of a car, coach or even train?

The answer is a complex one, and relates to the wider values of our civilization. For almost every generation in these islands except perhaps the last one, and indeed for much of the population of the planet to this very day, walking is the only available form of transport. If you want to go anywhere you walk, whether it is to the next village or across a continent.

Only since the Industrial Revolution have people had the freedom deliberately to shun coach or car in favour of walking, and in recent decades this has become a wide popular movement, with walking now established as the single most popular outdoor recreational activity in the United Kingdom. We walk to improve our health, to awaken our interest in the world around us and to escape the artificiality of modern life. The habit of rambling, indeed, owes a great deal to the Romantic and post-Romantic poets, the post-Wordsworthians who have taught us to feel suitable veneration before mountains, and that somewhat nebulous concept of "nature". The very notion of countryside, as a kind of ever-changing harmonious back-cloth for leisure activity, is essentially an urban concept, and one which the genuine countryman sometimes finds hard to understand.

But, in a highly technical civilization, country rambling has even more essential purposes. We live in an era of sensory deprivation, when much of our information reaches us, through film, television, videotape, word processor and microchip, in a highly artificial form. We learn of distant wars, the deaths of presidents, economic collapse, through the ordering of dots upon a glass screen. We live out our lives in centrally heated rooms, artificially lit offices, warm cars, scarcely aware of the changing of the seasons. Reality is something seen dimly and distantly through steamed-up windows.

Nothing illustrates this better than our preoccupation with that curse and blessing of our civilization, the car. The car places a screen of glass between us and the real world. The world flashes past like images on a television screen, a procession at forty or fifty miles an hour, confined to the modern highway. At the end of the day the experience is as instantly forgettable as last night's television programme.

Yet when you can persuade yourself to leave the comfort of the vehicle, you enter a different mode of being. The rhythm of your own muscles determines your speed of perception. You are made aware of the physical shape of the land – a valley, a hillock, a mound, a crag. You know again the feel of the wind in your face, the fresh smell of earth, the acid tang of oak-woods; the sound of becks boiling after rain, the dissonant bleat of sheep on the fellside, the hauntingly sad call of a curlew circling above you. You see again the detail previously passed in a blur – grass, rocks, pebbles, lichen. Nor can you easily forget the sheer animal pleasure of physical exertion after a ramble which gives way to a healthy exhaustion, a sense of well-being that is difficult to describe.

For in truth rambling is a sensuous experience, an opportunity to return to simpler, truer ways of perceiving our environment, knowing it as medieval, Renaissance or even eighteenth-century man knew it, a larger, subtler, more complex world than the clichés of modern packaged travel allow. To walk across a land-scape is to rediscover its vastness.

It is no accident that many ramblers, whilst enjoying walking for its own sake, use it as a means to pursue related interests. Many keen walkers in the Dales – from the time of Adam Sedgwick and John Phillips onwards, have been keen naturalists and geologists, ornithologists or botanists, archaeologists or historians. Not surprisingly there is a distinguished literature of the Dales reflecting these interests.

There are too, many excellent "field guides" for ramblers in the Dales in existence.

By field guide I mean the type of book to be carried in an anorak or rucksack pocket which gives precise, detailed advice, in words, by maps, or a combination of the two, to take the walker from stile to stile. These are valuable and useful tools for anyone wishing to explore the area on foot, and I have no wish to supplant them.

This book starts where the field guides leave off. It will attempt to take a broader view of the region from a walker's point of view, to help see the available field guides in context, to help anyone planning a trip or series of trips to the Dales to try and improve the quality of the experience.

I hope, too, it may find space on the bookshelf of the armchair rambler. We are all, at various times in our lives, armchair ramblers. This may be because of age or infirmity, circumstances of various kinds, or indeed that the prospect of a wild afternoon on the fells in December is a more arduous one than our inclination can cope with. Rain blowing from the north-east horizontally makes cowards of us all. It may, for the *cognoscenti*, strike a few discords or even cause sense of outrage if I get the facts wrong; as J. B. Priestley has pointed out in his *English Journey*, there is a very special and intimate relationship between the old industrial West Riding and the Yorkshire Dales and I tread literally upon hallowed ground.

Not that this book is in any sense only for the dedicated fell walker and bog-trotter. Far from it; may the timid and the uninitiated be tempted away from the security of their homes and the comfort of their cars. You do not have to begin a love-affair with the Yorkshire Dales in waist-high bracken and calf-deep bogs; gentle riversides exist to cajole those with but a spark of soul and flicker of initiative.

In so doing I run another risk. Many of my farming friends and neighbours would prefer that such newcomers were told that, in the Dales, it is always raining, the beer thin and the scenery dull, because "there's enough folk about already". But other neighbours, shopkeepers, publicans and café proprietors would hardly agree, needing a good few more visitors to make ends meet.

Both groups would agree that what they need is more people who know what they are about and who will give to the area as much as they take.

So I have no option but to tell the truth; that walking in the Dales is a bit like love, good wine, good food and fine music – aspects of human experience you do not miss if you have never enjoyed them. But once you have, you will need no further persuasion.

2

The Yorkshire Dales

Let us first of all try and see the Yorkshire Dales in a wider, a European, context. There are indeed regions with more spectacular mountains, lakes, forests; with dramatic sea coasts, richer flora and fauna, with a superb climate and perhaps even prettier villages. Compared with the great highland and mountainous regions of Europe, the Dales are a very small area indeed.

Perhaps the greatest quality the region has, in its very small area, is a remarkable balance of contrasting elements, elements that create a landscape of remarkable harmony. England, one of the most densely populated and culturally rich countries in the world, contains landscape which at its best is an intimate landscape, small in scale but dense in meanings, a countryside that reflects a long continuity of human occupation, and, at least in the past, a balance between man and nature.

The Yorkshire Dales are England in microcosm. Nature has, through geological accident, juxtaposed mountain and valley landscapes into a small area; man has enriched and diversified the natural environment to a degree where it is impossible, on even a short afternoon's stroll, not to be aware of the centuries of human occupation around you. The landscape is the culture, the culture is the people.

Where are the Yorkshire Dales?

Take a map of the Pennines, that range of surprisingly bleak and wild hills, however modest they appear in height, that runs down the spine of northern England. Look at the major lines of communication that cross the central Pennines. Take an area starting at the Aire Gap, that ancient and natural pass across Britain and dominated by the old town of Skipton and include in this area everything up to the equivalent pass that divides the northern Pennines, the Stainmore Gap, now dominated by the

A66 and the towns of Brough and Barnard Castle. To the west look to the Vale of Lune now roughly followed by the West Coast Main-Line Railway (Euston–Glasgow) and the M6 motorway; to the east follow the moorlands that finally peter out in the Vale of Mowbray and the Vale of York, with a line roughly from Barnard Castle and Richmond, Masham, Ripon, Pateley and Otley. The area does not follow the nonsense of local government boundaries that, would you believe it, has half the Howgill Fells in the National Park and half out, that excludes such glorious areas from the park as Mallerstang, Wild Boar Fell, Middleton and Leck Fell, and Upper Nidderdale. Such boundaries are at best an irrelevance, at worst a nuisance. The best guide is how people choose to describe themselves, whether or not they describe the villages they live in as "the Dales". In fact the region does have a remarkable geographic unity and sense of identity in the same way that, for example, on a larger scale the Tyrol (divided between Austria and Italy) does, or the Basque country in the Pyrenees.

No one would claim that the Dales region has a good climate. The official phrase is "maritime" which simply means that, like the Lake District, depressions come straight off the Irish Sea to empty their contents onto the western-facing hills. When it rains in the Dales, which is often, it comes like stair-rods, frequently sideways, driven by a westerly gale. The higher you are the more rigorous the climate; over a thousand feet it can be as fiercesome as anywhere in England, with snow coming early and lying late, frosts late in spring and early in autumn. The westerly, and higher areas get most rain, the eastern dales are comparatively dry, though in the worst winters, when blizzards drive from the north and east, the west may escape comparatively lightly whilst drifts as high as houses obliterate villages in the east. In the terrible winter of 1978–9 one minor road between Wensleydale and Swaledale remained blocked from December until May. Householders in remoter farms and hamlets must, as a matter of course, ensure they have a week or so supplies of food in at the start of the winter.

Yet, after days of cloud and gloom, the weather can change into a day of brilliance, with often dramatic effects of cloud and sun, as in the Lake District, giving stunning effects of light, like a painting by Turner at his most eloquent, that can be thrilling if you are on the fells. When that rare anticyclone does hover, calm and still above, the weather can be hot enough for one to walk stripped to the waist or in a thin shirt on the fells, and a swiftly flowing beck becomes a respite of coolness and refreshment. On such days walks have to be timed to start and finish at the appropriate tavern or café.

And yet, equally, the weather can change from clear, crystal blue to a maelstrom in a matter of minutes. Thunderstorms are not uncommon at any time of the year, and, aided by the upcurrents from the hills, can explode in frenzy. But mild, hazy, gentle days, even in the middle of winter, can make it a joy to be alive and in the Pennines.

In essence, Dales weather is like the weather for the rest of England to an exaggerated degree: fickle, exceptionally changeable, but when good, simply glorious.

Understanding of the landscape must begin with the bedrock. The major part of the Yorkshire Dales consists of various kinds of rock of the Carboniferous era, sedimentary rocks, sandstones, gritstones, shales and spectacular limestones, laid down in vast primeval estuaries and shallow, lagoon-like seas some 300 to 400 million years ago. The huge convulsions and contractions that created most of the major mountain ranges of Europe also had the effect of thrusting up the ancient underlying granites that form the Askrigg Block until the pressures on the earth's crust produced the gigantic splitting and faulting in the west and south of the Dales. This in turn revealed the underlying layers of rock like the slices of some gargantuan cake.

To develop the metaphor of the cake; it is as if this huge layer-cake of gritstones, limestones, sandstones and shales was tilted down towards the east, with, along the fault lines to the south-west, spectacular escarpments where the crags and scars were formed that make the Dales famous. Erosion by ice, by rivers and by primeval snows has, over millennia, carved the steep-sided Dales out of the layer-cake, to leave the isolated flat-topped fells with their smooth summits, often rounded by the glaciers, as the free-standing fells or peaks, all remarkably uniform in height. The summits are capped by the harder gritstones and are often stepped in appearance as softer shales have worn away more quickly than the harder Yoredale limestones that jut out as defiant crags.

Glaciation, too, has carved the valleys out more steeply, creating many of the steep little gills and waterfalls that hurtle down the valley sides. There are more waterfalls in the Dales than in any other area in England.

Indeed, water plays a remarkably important part in the landscape of the Dales, even though there are only two natural lakes, Semerwater and Malham Tarn, of any significant size. Everywhere are sikes (natural drainage channels), streamlets, becks, and rivers, draining from high moorland bogs and mosses. The rivers can rise after a storm or with melting snow, with sudden and alarming speed and with a ferocity which can be both frightening and dangerous. After a period of heavy rain everywhere gleams and glistens and gurgles with the movement of water; best of all if bright sunlight then catches at the white crests of waterfalls or foaming becks – the effect can be quite exhilarating.

The water often suddenly vanishes out of sight, or reappears, a surging torrent, from the middle of nowhere. Not for nothing were the Dales, at their time of fashionable discovery in the later eighteenth century, almost called the Cave District, for the region is virtually hollow, riddled with hundreds of miles of caves and underground passages, gouged out by the abrasive action of rain-water, limestones dissolved by the acidity of the surface runoff. The true glories of the Pennines underground can only really be experienced by the pot-holer, properly equipped and with an experienced team; the more nervous or cautious visitor can have some inkling of the richness and variety of this hidden underworld through a visit to one of the show caves in the area such as White Scar, Ingleton, Ingleborough Cave, Clapham or Stump Cross on the road between Grassington and Pateley Bridge.

But the fell walker can often experience something of the grandeur of the world of the pot-holer where the underworld and the outside world meet – the great, yawning chasms or pot-holes which the early Romantic travellers saw as entrances into hell, or, as described in later sections of this book, by walking through a collapsed chasm or narrow gorge where cliff and crag give an impression of subterranean magnificence.

The power of water can often be seen too where rivers and becks have cut deeply into and underneath the Carboniferous limestones, creating strange and beautiful formations – over-hangs, whirlpools, sculptured shapes reminiscent of the work of the great Henry Moore – significantly a Yorkshireman.

The north-western corner of the Dales belongs, geologically, to the Lake District, being, west of the Dent Fault that divides the Pennines from the Lake District, of even more ancient Silurian and Ordovician rocks, ancient slates and flagstones that form the smooth, rounded domes of the Howgill Fells. These older rocks appear, too, in a narrow band further south around Ingleton and in Ribblesdale, where quarries work these ancient rocks for roadstone. Some, around Ingleton, are even older, amongst the most ancient and mysterious rocks known in the United Kingdom.

Rocks determine the soils which carry the vegetation, the "green mantle" of the Dales. In limestone areas the soil is thin but alkaline, producing sweet pastures and a rich, sub-Alpine flora; the gritstone moorlands have an acid soil, an acidity increased by centuries of grazing and the leaching out of nutrients by heavy rain and snowfall, producing on the higher moorlands to the west near tundra conditions of sphagnum bog, peat-hags and cotton-grass, and in the drier east heath and heather moorland. The valley bottoms carry diluvian clays and gravel, often built up into huge glacial moraines by the retreating ice, to produce the most fertile soils and the most important areas for farming, with fertile meadows.

Man's effect on the natural landscape has been profound. Originally, at least in post-Ice Age times, the Dales were thickly wooded, with forests of birch, pine, hazel, elm and oak. The coming of men, the early Mesolithic hunters some 8,000 years ago, began to alter the balance of nature. It would appear that tribes from what is now continental Europe crossed into northern Britain, then attached to the mainland, for summer hunting of deer and wild boar. Many hundreds of spear- and arrow-heads and tools found in the Pennines attest to the scale of this activity.

The severance of Britain from the continental landmass around 6400 BC led to increasing pressure on the ecosystem and the human population permanently resident in these islands in-creased. Neolithic man became a farmer, at first with stone tools and later with the new bronze and iron technologies imported from the Continent with successive waves of invaders, and the clearance of the primeval Dales forest began. Archaeologists can now, through pollen-dating techniques, assess just when these upland clearances began, as man created space on the well-drained limestone plateaux for his huts and enclosures to keep beasts and grow cereal. The latest archaeological evidence suggests that in Iron Age times man was remarkably self-sufficient, already beginning the tradition of pastoral farming on the upland that still continues, perhaps even managing the woodland that provided fuel and building material, communicating by ancient tracks and trade routes that kept to the edges of the moorland to avoid the bog and scrub of the valleys.

By the time of the Roman Conquest of Britain the Dales were part of a well-organized and prosperous federation of tribes known as the Brigantes who for many years led bitter resistance against the invading legions, as evidenced by hill-forts on Ingleborough and in Grass Wood and defensive fortifications at Tor Dyke, Wharfedale, Fremington, Swaledale and Stanwick, where in AD 74 the Brigantian leader, Venutius, was finally crushed by Julius Agricola's superb army. But it would appear that the Romans' grip on the western half of Brigantia was far from secure; only one villa-farm is known in the Dales at Gargrave, suggesting that the colonists preferred milder and friendlier climes, and despite a major fort at Ilkley, a smaller one at Bainbridge, and a campaigning road between the two still visible across the Stake Pass above Buckden, and from Bainbridge to Ribchester over Cam Fell, the Romans preferred to keep well clear of the Dales. Only the lead veins to the east attracted them, and there is some evidence of Roman mining activity in the Greenhow area.

It would be nice to imagine a continuity of tradition between the Celtic Brigantian peoples and the present-day self-reliant Dalesman who still does not take too kindly to interfering outsiders. But more likely the Dalesman's true ancestors are the successive generations of Angles and Danes from the east and Vikings from the west who chopped, burned and hacked the scrubland from the valley bottoms and established the farmsteads, hamlets and villages we know today by corrupted forms of their names, suffixed by tun, ley, thwaite or holme. History will never tell us the complex history of conquest and counter-conquest, and perhaps the ensuing pattern of verbal treaty and eventual co-operation and intermarriage that resulted in communities emerging often tightly organized around village centres in Anglian and

Danish areas, but more scattered among Viking settlements, for example in Garsdale and Dentdale. A large-scale map of the Yorkshire Dales with its dense interweaving of Old English and Old Norse place-names is a kind of register of those early struggles for land, the Vikings from their kingdom-colony of Dublin in particular, often penetrating the wildest and loneliest of dale heads, as if driven by some folk memory of Scandinavian fiord or dale-head fringes.

They have left their voice in the language too; the harsh, clipped grammar of Dales dialect, never using two words if one will do, the economy and even wit of Dales speech, much common Norse vocabulary, often incomprehensible to southern Englishmen but familiar to Scandinavians. Dialect survives in spite of the inroads of modern technological civilization.

To a great degree, therefore, the Dales around the time of the Norman Conquest must have begun to take on the appearance we would now recognize. The valleys would be settled, the forest in retreat, wooden villages and farms occupying the identical sites we see today, a language spoken in those farms which, if we could not immediately understand it, would have enough in common with our own speech to be, in time, intelligible to us. The farming would not, of course, be entirely pastoral as today; such specialization is only the result of modern industrial civilization. The Angles in particular farmed from open fields, shared in common, divided up into narrow cultivatable terraces on the hillsides called "lynchets" or "reins" that remained in use for the cultivation of grain right up to the beginning of last century, and which can still be seen throughout the Dales, particularly after a light snowfall or in the long light of evening or mid-winter.

Every later generation has, to a degree, imposed its own script on this basic pattern established by the Anglian settlers. Many of the footpaths suggested in this book trace out the exact ways and paths between farmsteads, between settlements, to the site of the pagan temple, later Christianized, used by our ancestors, more than a thousand years ago. Some of these old ways have over succeeding centuries become ever more important: cart roads, waggon ways, carriage roads, and finally modern motor roads, widened, surfaced and improved out of all recognition. But others have remained much as the Angles knew them, traced out by centuries of feet and hooves, marking the continuity of man on these islands.

The Normans, for example, imposed their own authoritarian structure upon the Dales, built castles at key points such as Richmond, Sedbergh, Skipton and developed new administrative structures that required new roads, new market centres. Areas were set aside in Wharfedale and Wensleydale as hunting forests or reserves, where the once common red deer could be chased. Lodges were built where the nobles could shelter and seek entertainment. Barden Tower in Wharfedale was originally just such a place.

The great monastic houses, including the Cistercians at Fountains Abbey and the Augustinian Canons at Bolton Priory laid the foundations of the great Yorkshire wool industry with a system of outlying granges to manage land given or bequeathed to them over many generations. Great flocks of sheep roamed the uplands, wool was exported to the new merchant states of Renaissance Italy, and the wealth of the trade helped to build the great abbey on the Skell at Fountains, and the majestic priory on the Wharfe at Bolton, so beloved by Turner, Wordsworth, Ruskin and Landseer as a picturesque ruin. It also helped to establish York as England's second city where merchandise found its way to and from the Continent.

Many monastic ways and tracks remain in the Dales, perhaps the most famous of them being Mastiles Lane, connecting up lands owned by Fountains in the Lake District, Ribblehead and Malhamdale with the important grange at Kilnsey, before flocks of sheep and produce continued over the Wharfe to Nidderdale and Fountains. A tiny fraction of the gatehouse to the original grange still survives just in front of the Jacobean Old Hall at Kilnsey.

The growing wealth of the country in Tudor and Jacobean times led to the rebuilding of many old Dales farmhouses into the form we see today, the traditional Dales langhouse with barn and farm all under one continuous roof, and in later centuries in more modern styles. It is likely that the skills of masons trained in the great monastic houses were kept alive by the increase in secular building in the Dales in the sixteenth and seventeenth centuries, with many fine cottages and barns dating from this period, and lovely arched pack-horse bridges.

The Enclosure Acts of the eighteenth and nineteenth centuries led to further changes in the landscape, notably the miles of dry-stone walls like lines pencilled across the open fell, apportioning land to local farms and commoners; often the poorer people dispossessed by enclosure were taken on by the larger landowners to build the seemingly endless bands of stone crossing the fells at perilous angles. The pattern of scattered barns and dry-stone walls is a particular feature of the Dales landscape, and the careful observer can distinguish between the ancient medieval and Tudor enclosures, close to villages and farms and usually irregular, and the uniform, straight surveyor's lines of the enclosure period.

Interestingly enough many footpaths were specifically created at the time of enclosure to allow local residents and the public at large facilities for recreation, to compensate for loss of access to the open fellsides. So it is simply not true to say that footpaths were only created in the past for work and essential needs of communication.

Many areas of open common remain, however, in the Dales, some of these, for example Whernside or the Howgill Fells, extremely extensive. "Common" land does not mean common ownership; almost all land in the Dales is owned by someone. "Common" refers to specific rights of grazing, or turbary (fuel-gathering) by local householders or farmers. It does not even mean right to roam at will as on commons in urban areas or many parts of southern Britain. In practice many open areas of the Dales that are also commons, have a long-established traditional usage – or *de facto* access – that has allowed people to wander at will, providing of course they cause no disturbance or damage. In other areas, for example on Abbotside Common north of Hawes, the public has a legal right to wander at will but not to take a dog, and on the huge areas of Barden Moor and Barden Fell above Bolton Abbey in Wharfedale a special access agreement permits access by the public subject to certain conditions, except at times of shooting or high fire risk.

The Dales area had its share of the Industrial Revolution. Many mills were built, originally to grind the local corn, and driven by water-power from a beck or river. In later years they were converted to weave flax, cotton or wool, until driven out of business in the mid-nineteenth century as cheap coal, canal and rail transport made production in the industrial towns of west Yorkshire and south Lancashire more economic. Mass industry killed too, many of the Dales cottage industries, such as the home knitting which was an immensely strong tradition particularly in the northern Dales of Dentdale, Garsdale and Wensleydale.

One industry which did flourish for many years was lead mining. Lead had been worked in the Dales since Roman times, but as demand increased in the Tudor and Jacobean period, partnerships of free miners came into being to work the rich veins of ore in Wharfedale and Swaledale. Mechanization in the eighteenth and nineteenth centuries led to deeper shafts than the old bellpits, and complex and highly sophisticated engineering techniques to drain the deeper shafts and provide water-power to service the mines and the new smelt mills. By the mid-nineteenth century Dales mines were producing a substantial proportion of the country's requirements of lead and it is said, probably correctly, that a substantial proportion of the cost of Chatsworth House was obtained by the Duke of Devonshire from his mines on Grassington Moor.

Dwindling veins and cheap supplies of lead ore from Spain ended the industry in the Dales by the 1880s, and brought in a period of economic decline and misery only relieved by emigration and, in later years as branch railways were built, by tourism. But many Dales villages which we now, from a period of a century or more after their industry has declined, declare picturesque and photograph for calendars are, in essence, mining villages – Grassington, Hebden, Kettlewell, Reeth, Muker and Gunnerside are particular examples – with the tiny poky cottages and narrow, unhygienic courts and folds now lovingly restored by city people seeking a "period" cottage in the country away from the urban sprawl. History has its delicate ironies.

The only industry, apart from agriculture, to survive on any scale in the Dales is quarrying. The hundreds of small roadside sandstone quarries used for building the walls, barns and cottages are no longer in use nor are even the larger quarries and stone mines that grew up in the Hawes district after the collapse of lead mining to provide cheap stone, carried by rail, for the new cotton towns of south Lancashire. Dales quarries are now almost entirely limestone, except for Silurian flags used for roadstone in the Ingleton and Helwith Bridge areas. They are controlled by multi-national corporations, and provide building and construction stone for the entire region, as well as vital limestone for the steel industry. They remain an important source of local employment in the Dales, even if they do little to improve the scenery. But their future is threatened by the present economic recession.

Farming in the Dales still remains surprisingly traditional, with stock-rearing and dairy cattle (the ubiquitous black and white Friesian to be seen on most lower farms) and sheep providing the main part of the Dales farmer's livelihood. The two traditional Dales breeds of black-faced mountain sheep, ferociously hardy, the Swaledale and the Dalesbred still dominate the upland pastures and the high fells, though more exotic creatures intrude for breeding purposes. The tendency for ranch farming is not yet as pronounced as in many areas of Britain, although farming in the Dales is much less labour intensive than it was a few years ago, with often a man and his son tackling a farm, or even two or more farms that perhaps a dozen men with horses could not cope with only a generation ago. New cowhouses behind the farm may not be as picturesque as the scattered, traditional barns, but if they save the farmer a couple of hours' work a day, beauty may have its price in human terms. For farming is not very secure in the Dales. Many economists would argue that it does not "pay" to have a small family unit farm high up in the Dales. You do not make a fortune out of hill farming. Farmers do it for other reasons – because they love farming, and their land, their beasts and the Dales. Some are owner-occupiers and others are tenants, often with landlords who might just as easily sell the land and live in the Canary Isles on the interest, but would prefer to see a young man and his wife make a go of it in spite of the difficult climatic conditions, the many hardships and privations, the long hours, and weeks when blizzards isolate you from the rest of civilization. Of course there are plenty of shrewd and careful farmers who are worth – at least on paper – a modest fortune. They are proud, resourceful, self-made men, and they are the true guardians of the Dales countryside. Without their care and concern, ability to drain the pastures, repair the walls, plant shelter-belts, tidy the farmyard, restore those traditional buildings, the natural beauty we venerate so much would quickly vanish, and Dales communities, deprived of their essential life-blood, become retreats of the well-to-do and the geriatric.

The greatest threat to the Dales farmer comes from outside forces, changes in agricultural and farming policy, EEC regulations and new fiscal measures. Much as they value their independence, it is, at the end of the day, an illusion, and depends on governments recognizing their special needs. One particular threat lies with commercial afforestation which, though it reflects a dramatic change in land use, is for historic reasons outside planning control. Forestry is no more "economic" than growing figs or dates in the Dales; it depends for its survival in the Dales on huge tax incentives and grants, given for wider strategic reasons. Once forestry becomes more commercially attractive than farming, or in other words once governments tip the economic scales in that particular way, the open Dales hillsides and the farming communities are doomed.

Not that forestry does not have an important place in the Dales. Much of the original tree cover needs returning, but the emphasis needs to be on the original native species – pine, hazel, rowan, oak, birch – which do not figure highly in the modern commercial forestry business. What the Dales needs is not large-scale commercial planting of sitka spruce but more amenity woodlands of mixed species including hardwoods, on a smaller scale, rather than the cash crop of sitka. The government has merely to change the rules to make this kind of afforestation more viable.

Whether or not commercial afforestation poses a threat to the natural habitat is a difficult question. Some people would argue that increased tree cover would, at least whilst the trees are young, increase the variety of habitats especially for bird life. Others point to the deadening effect of monoculture spruce production which, unlike the selectively felled mixed forests of, say, the Swiss or Austrian Alps, do not offer the mixture of light and shade in which a variety of species can flourish. Fortunately it is likely that the least interesting moorlands, overgrazed, acid land full of rushes and bent, of little botanic or agricultural value, will offer the most obvious sites for forestry, and it is hoped that agreement between the Forestry Commission, private forestry concerns and the National Park Authority who are currently preparing a Forestry Policy Map, will ensure that afforestation occurs in ways which do not seriously affect agriculture or natural history.

The naturalist, indeed, has much to delight him or her. The

richest areas are the limestone uplands, especially where for a variety of reasons, intensive grazing has not occurred. This may be in some of the relict woodlands, fragments of the ancient forests that cling to some steep hanging valley, or up on the extensive tracts of limestone pavement where because of the difficulties and dangers, sheep have been excluded; or in the steep and narrow gills where sheep and cattle cannot easily get and a spray-filled beckside allows luxurious ferns to flourish; or even in old forgotten quarry and spoil tips on whose alkaline wastes orchids and tway-blades multiply.

Among the more common but delightful flowers to be found on the limestone are purple orchids, primroses, violets, cowslips, rock-roses, saxifrages, the beautiful little bird's-eye primrose and cranesbill. The high moorlands are less rich, but the vivid splash of yellow and purple mountain pansies makes an unforgettable sight in spring, and on the drier moors to the east, so does the rich expanse of heather and ling, sweetly scented and crimson purple in late summer. The meadows and hedgerows are richly streaked with buttercup, clover, campion, ragged robin, blue cranesbill, vetches and water avens, whilst the woods offer a haze of bluebell, ransoms, wood sorrel and wood anemones in spring that delight all but the most prosaic.

The Dales are not rich in trees, but the ash, holly, hazel and rowan are especially distinctive on the uplands, with the intense scarlet rowan-berries in the autumn one of the most thrilling sights. Oak prefers the more acid gritstones, and some splendid, ancient specimens grace the Bolton Abbey area. Beech, wych-elm and sycamore are much in evidence in the lower dales, whilst alder and willow occupy the riverbanks and becksides. Many of the larger estates in the last century introduced new species, including the more exotic conifers, so it always requires a little care to distinguish between the native tree and the newer immigrant.

The Dales are also noted for bird life. This varies, like the landscape, according to height and tree cover. The curlew must be the most dramatic and instantly recognizable bird of the high moorlands, its curved bill and cry quite unmistakable. Plovers, snipe, black-headed gulls, kestrels, and many of the rarer birds of prey are often to be seen on the high fells whilst black and the native red grouse dominate the heather moors. The riversides attract dipper, wagtails, sandpipers, mallard, kingfishers, martins and swallows, whilst larger stretches of water, such as Malham Tarn, Barden Reservoirs and the Gouthwaite Reservoir in Nidderdale, now a nature reserve, attract many attractive birds of passage including whooper and Bewick's swans, Canada geese, golden-eye and the common scoter.

Skylarks are common enough in the higher meadows, together with fieldfares, gulls, owls and magpies, whilst in the woodlands you may be lucky enough to see and hear the woodpecker, as well as innumerable finches, robins, tits, blackbirds, flycatchers and perhaps nuthatches.

One of the most thrilling sights of all on a ramble is to see a heron lazily flapping up some steep moorland gill, ready to lunge at a trout or grayling.

Mammals require more care for a sighting. Grey and, occasionally, red squirrels are often evident in woodland. Hares are common enough, especially when foraging in the winter months, their graceful leaps high enough to clear a stone wall. Rabbits have in recent years made a dramatic come-back after the effects of myxomatosis, and on a typical ramble you are quite likely to see a stoat, a weasel or a common vole. Foxes are fairly numerous, but generally detect people before people detect them, whilst badgers, who have one or two strongholds in the Dales, are generally only seen by patient watchers at the sets. Deer, once common in the Dales, are making a reappearance, with sightings recorded by the occasional startled motorist. These have doubtless found their way down from afforested areas to the north or across from Bowland and might, if an enterprising landowner decided upon such a course of action, eventually re-establish themselves in the Yorkshire Dales.

It goes without saying perhaps, that the rambler should always take care to cause the minimum disturbance to habitats, particularly nests or sets. Wild flowers once picked are destroyed and it is worth remembering that the picking and uprooting of many plants in this country is illegal, though it does not require the force of law to make a civilized person understand that our environment is precious and needs the active protection of every individual if our successors are going to have anything worthwhile to enjoy. Conservation, like many things, is an attitude of mind rather than a series of regulations.

A major force of change in the Dales is tourism. Tourism is a complex and emotional subject, but really involves many different aspects. Its roots lie firmly in the Industrial Revolution and the destruction of the natural environment which came from rapid urbanization. The Dales region, because of its isolation, missed much of the second part of the Industrial Revolution, remaining predominantly rural and unspoiled.

The early refugees from the Industrial Revolution were the travellers and poets, the painters and, later, photographers who between them gave us certain attitudes towards the countryside and to nature which, if we think about such things at all, we call "Romantic". In particular the Romantic poets whose disciples wrote the guidebooks, designed the railway posters and produced the calendars, taught the newly literate inhabitants of the cities that mountains were places to seek for solitude and beauty, that Dales scenery was "picturesque". The Victorians' love of wild flowers and of geology allowed their successors to see a region like the Dales as a storehouse of beauty and knowledge. Later scientists and scholars have helped to identify many things that are important and precious in a habitat not totally dominated by man's recent activities.

So visitors came, initially by carriage and on horseback, then in larger numbers by train, by bus and finally, in an avalanche of cars. They came from the factories and mills of nearby West Riding, from south Lancashire and Teesside. They came for the day, or to stay a week in one of the new guest-houses or hotels, or farmhouses offering bed and breakfast. Or they came to stay permanently, from all over Britain, because they had lived all their lives in a noisy, frenzied city or faceless suburb and now they had retired with a little money and time to enjoy it. Or they came because they were a writer, a potter or a painter, and stayed to write, pot or paint.

They have changed the Dales profoundly. They have brought new industry – cafés, workshops and hotels. They have helped older businesses which, in the nature of things would have closed or vanished, to survive and even expand. Bookshops, cobblers, pubs, even grocers and chemists now rely on the annual influx of pound notes to make their lives more agreeable. Money has been put into the local economy. Cottages which would have collapsed in ruins are now rebuilt, restored – giving work, incidentally, to local men who would have otherwise have had to leave for Coventry or Doncaster.

Of course there is a less welcome side to all this.

The Dales are in danger of becoming a one-class society, a society of professional, business and tradespeople, people who may have much to offer the community and will sit on committees, sing in choirs and organize the WI outing. But a young working-class couple who may be lucky enough to have work in the area may find themselves outbid for a modest cottage by a solicitor from Birmingham who only wants the cottage for occasional weekend use, or a property developer who will put in central heating and offer it as a "self-catering cottage" for the summer. Villages, full of visitors in the summer, empty out during the winter months. Schools close, buses run empty and are withdrawn, vital services are cut and life gets that much more difficult for the remaining members of the older agricultural community.

These are major problems but not insoluble given the will. But will the sheer pressure of visitors destroy the very beauty they seek? It was in order to resolve this dilemma, and to provide the facilities the urban majority required, that in 1949 the National Parks and Access to the Countryside Act was passed, and in 1954, 680 square miles (significantly 340 square miles in the old North Riding and 340 miles in the old West Riding) of the Yorkshire Dales were designated a National Park.

Few terms have caused more confusion than the name "National Park". Based on the American experience in the last century where stretches of virgin land were literally acquired for the nation, in Britain parks were imposed upon landscapes already owned, settled and worked by generations of local inhabitants. Perhaps a term such as "National Heritage Areas" might have been more appropriate. Britain's National Parks are not "national" in the sense of being nationally owned, neither are they "parks" in the usually accepted sense of the word.

In fact Britain's National Parks are a part of local government, except for the Lake District and the Peak which have independent boards. The Yorkshire Dales are controlled by a National Park Committee, a committee administered by North Yorkshire County Council. The twenty-four members of this committee are made up of twelve North Yorkshire county councillors, one Cumbria

county councillor (10 per cent of the park being in Cumbria), three district councillors from each district council involved, and eight people appointed by the Secretary of State to represent wider recreational, agricultural or conservation interests – the so-called national interest.

Although the elected local authority members retain overall control, finance comes in the largest measure from central Government, around 75 per cent of expenditure through what is known as the Rate Support Grant from the Department of the Environment, subject to the advice and guidance of the Countryside Commission, an independent Government agency.

The National Park has a full-time staff of around sixty, as well as seasonal and part-time staff. The headquarters are in Bainbridge with a subsiduary office in Grassington. The department, headed by National Park Officer Mr R. J. Harvey, carries out the policies of the National Park Committee who meet each month in Northallerton.

The major work of the National Park Committee involves development control. This ensures that any new development in the National Park area meets stringent requirements of materials, design and siting, and by this means it is possible to ensure that Dales villages are not drowned by ugly new developments that would clash with their surroundings and with existing buildings. A mark of excellence, it has been justly said, of new development in an area like the Dales, is that you should not notice a new house or converted barn, but assume it has always been there.

As well as ensuring new development is harmonious, the Dales Committee is in effect the local planning authority for the area. Caravan and camping sites are permitted only in chosen localities, and sites are screened. Local plans are prepared to ensure that the future of the area is determined by pre-agreed criteria and not by chance. Motor rallies are, in liaison with the RAC and police, strictly controlled.

Much of this is what might be termed "negative planning" and not popular. None of us like to be planned. Other people cause traffic congestion not ourselves; our new building or extension is not an eyesore, our neighbour's is. Decisions are often controversial and professional staff can, ultimately, only advise politicians and not take the decisions. Planning mistakes may survive for generations, successes are simply not noticed. It is a difficult, demanding job but without it the Dales would, within a single generation, be ruined for ever.

On a more positive note, the Park Authority spends a good deal of time and energy on conserving the environment. Trees (only native to the Dales) are planted, eyesores removed, grants given to restore old but important buildings; help is given for archaeology and industrial archaeology, and for nature conservation. One excellent improvement in recent years has been an increased involvement with the local community over the Upland Management Scheme, whereby a Dales farmer faced with a broken wall, smashed stile or just genuine wear and tear is given a grant to make the damage good, using his own labour, a local craftsman, or one of the park's own team of skilled field assistants. This has resulted in a quite dramatic improvement in the standard of maintenance of footpaths within the National Park area, a fact which walkers will quickly realize as fine new wooden signposts, new stiles and wicket gates make path finding and negotiation very much easier. A good deal of waymarking has also been completed, with the standard yellow and blue arrows or blobs helping to identify where the paths run. This makes things very much easier for the rambler, and it also solves problems for the farmer, reducing accidental trespass and damage.

This work has developed, through the field services, into a number of major projects which have utilized voluntary labour. New foot-bridges have been built, sections of eroded footpath replaced or restored, much of the work due to the efforts of young people from schools or youth groups working with the full-time warden service to achieve some dramatic results.

The team of National Park wardens remains the key people in such work, acting as the liaison between the public, the local farmer and the National Park Committee. Each full-time warden is responsible for an area of the park, and is assisted at weekends and holiday times by paid part-time assistants who patrol the major access areas and popular sites, keeping an eye on areas of visitor pressure and helping to reduce conflict between the less thoughtful kind of visitor and the farming community.

Walkers have every reason to feel a debt of gratitude to the warden service for the high standard of work on Dales footpaths and the very much improved relations with Dales farmers that have resulted.

Another important aspect of the National Park's work is the information service. National Park Centres are open at weekends and during the main holiday periods at Grassington, Aysgarth, Malham, Clapham, Sedbergh, and Hawes, adjacent to the main car parks, and as well as interesting interpretive displays about aspects of the National Park, the centres contain a full range of maps and literature about the park, including self-guided walks leaflets. The centre staff are mainly local people with a detailed knowledge of the area, and can often provide invaluable advice about facilities and things to see in the locality. Guided walks begin from centres throughout the season, and a leaflet is obtainable at centres giving full details.

But what about areas of the Dales outside the National Park area? These areas inevitably do not receive the same resources; paths are less well maintained, stiles are often rickety, signposting less common. Bradford, which has an energetic countryside team, perhaps achieves most in the Ilkley and Addingham areas, but outside the park in North Yorkshire, resources are spread rather thinly as they are in Lancashire and Cumbria. In these areas local authorities can take advantage of generous Countyside Commission grants for footpath maintenance and other work, but shortage of resources has meant that little more than minimal maintenance work has been achieved.

Local authorities and central Government are not the only bodies concerned with recreational provision in the countryside. Many voluntary bodies contribute a significant element to the conservation, management and enjoyment of the Yorkshire Dales. The National Trust owns a substantial area of limestone upland including and surrounding Malham Tarn, with its Tarn House Field Centre, where the Field Studies Council offers a range of fascinating courses in natural history, archaeology and related subjects. Details can be obtained from the Warden, Malham Tarn Field Centre, Settle, North Yorkshire. The National Trust employs its own warden in Malham and carefully nurtures the ecological variety and complexity of the area, attempting to prevent changes that would ruin a unique habitat.

The Society for the Promotion of Nature Conservation and the Yorkshire Naturalists' Trust manage a number of important sites in the Dales, in conjunction with the Nature Conservancy Council the national body who provide advice and a degree of finance for such purposes. Ownership of such sites is, in the long term, the only way to protect the most precious areas. More than a fifth of the National Park area is registered as various Sites of Special Scientific Interest. The enthusiasm and expertise of these voluntary groups has done much to ensure the protection and conservation of these unique habitats, and with them the flowers, the bird life and the wild mammals that are so important. To find out more about the trust's work and sites in Yorkshire, write to them at 20 Castlegate, York YO1 1RP.

Protection of the countryside on a wider scale is undertaken by a number of bodies, most notably the Council for the Protection of Rural England, that has branches in Craven and Wensleydale; information about local activity can be obtained from the CPRE at 4, Hobart Place, London SW1W 0HY. The Ramblers' Association is active not only in footpath matters in the Dales, but in acting, with CPRE, as a watch-dog over amenity matters. The RA, through its area branches, organizes regular walks in the Yorkshire Dales, using public transport, members' own transport or specially chartered coaches. As well as in the nearby big towns, active groups based on Skipton, Richmond and Lancaster keep a special watch on Dales footpaths. No serious walker should fail to join the Ramblers' Association which has done much to protect the rights of the ordinary walker in the countryside, through constant vigilance at a local level, and pressure to achieve effective footpath and National Park legislation at national level. The address of the association is 1–5 Wandsworth Road, London SW8 2LJ.

Caving, whilst being of less direct interest to the walker, is undertaken by a number of specialist pot-holing and speleological groups in the region, represented by the Council of Northern Caving Clubs, 24 High Street, Skipton, North Yorkshire. It is significant that in the Yorkshire Dales, which have the most extensive natural cave system in the United Kingdom, is situated the country's national caving centre at Whernside Manor in Dentdale, now run by the Yorkshire Dales National Park Committee in and from a splendid old country house under the shadow of Whernside, under the direction of the warden, M. K. "Ben" Lyon, himself a caver of international repute. As well as running caving courses at every level from absolute beginners to the most technically sophisticated, the centre runs a number of

courses for fell walkers which provide the best possible introduction to the countryside, the geology, archaeology and natural history of the area as well as fundamentals of fellcraft. A postcard to the Whernside Cave and Fell Centre, Dent, Sedbergh, Cumbria, will bring full details of current courses which are offered at remarkably economic cost.

A similar venture, this time based on hotel, guest-house and even self-catering holidays in Wharfedale, is the Dales Centre, Grassington, North Yorkshire BD23 5AU, whose director, Terry Parker, has, with the support of the Countryside Commission, developed walking and educational holidays based on detailed discovery of the local and natural history of the area. A postcard to the Dales Centre will again bring full details of current courses.

No account of the interpretation of the Dales heritage would be complete without reference to the work of the Dalesman Publishing Company whose regular monthly magazine has done so much to establish the identity of the area, and whose list of specialized paperbacks on so much of Dales history and topography can be obtained direct from Dalesman, Clapham, via Lancaster.

Nor too, should one neglect to mention a number of very significant local museums whose collections and interpretive displays offer great insight into the history of the Yorkshire Dales. These include the Craven Museum in the Town Hall, Skipton, with its major collection of material relating to Craven, including the John Crowther collection from Grassington, and much material relating to natural history and lead mining. This is open daily except for Tuesdays and Sundays. The Upper Dales Folk Museum in Hawes contains the collection of Dales bygones belonging to the Dales historians and authors Marie Hartley and Joan Ingilby, and is now housed in the old railway warehouse in Hawes Station, and, run by North Yorkshire County Council, is open daily during the season.

Excellent smaller local museums exist at Reeth, which tells much of the story of local lead mining, Pateley Bridge with a good deal of material relating to Nidderdale, and at Grassington, where the Upper Wharfedale Museum Society has a superb collection of artefacts donated by many local people in the area and housed in former lead-miners' cottages in The Square. Settle boasts two museums – the splendid little "Pig Yard" collection which includes some major prehistoric remains found in Ribblesdale in the recent past, and the North Craven Heritage Trust Museum in Victoria Street which offers a quite superb interpretation of Craven's topography and history. A contrast is the Earby Mine Research Group's Museum of Mining which, whilst being outside the Dales area at School Lane, Earby, offers a unique insight into the lead-mining industry of the Wharfedale and Nidderdale areas, including sight of the great Kettlewell ore crusher, whilst rail enthusiasts will find a good deal to interest them at the Yorkshire Dales Railway at Embsay Station.

As the opening times of voluntary museums vary considerably as their resources and funds permit, look out for local publicity. The network of little Dales museums offers vividly rewarding insight into the area and, on those days when walking is at best unpleasant or perhaps even impossible, a pleasant and interesting trip out.

REFERENCE

The Pennine Dales, Arthur Raistrick (Eyre Methuen, 1968)
Old Yorkshire Dales, Arthur Raistrick (David & Charles, 1967)
Portrait of the Dales, Norman Duerden (Hale, 1979)
The Yorkshire Dales, Marie Hartley and Joan Ingilby (Dent, 1965)
Geology of the Yorkshire Dales, Peter R. Rodgers (Dalesman, 1978)
Mountains & Moorlands, W. H. Pearsall (Collins New Naturalist, Second Edition 1970)
The Naturalists' Yorkshire, Yorkshire Naturalists' Union (Dalesman, 1971)
Mountains & Moorlands, Arnold Darlington (Hodder & Stoughton, 1978)
Pennine Flowers, Joan Duncan and R. W. Robson (Dalesman, 1977)
Farming in Yorkshire, Bill Cowley (Dalesman, 1972)
Buildings in the Yorkshire Dales Arthur Raistrick (Dalesman, 1976)
Early Pennine Settlement, Alan King (Dalesman, 1970)
Monks and Shepherds in the Yorkshire Dales, Arthur Raistrick (Yorkshire Dales National Park, 1976)

Information on the Yorkshire Dales National Park can be obtained from the National Park Office, Hebden Road, Grassington, Skipton, North Yorkshire.

3

Some Practical Points

The joy of walking for pleasure lies in the fact that, in its initial
stages at least, rambling requires the minimum of special equipment and techniques. Most of us have a pair of feet and can walk.
Add to this old clothes (the Dales are no respecter of fashionable
fineries) and a decent pair of reasonably watertight shoes and the
Dales await you.

This assumes, naturally enough, that you are going no more
than a couple of miles on well-beaten tracks. Beyond this a little
more care might be needed.

Let us begin with the valley paths. Expect mud in the Yorkshire
Dales. If it is not raining it has been raining or it will be raining
soon so there is likely to be mud about. So even for short strolls of
five or six miles boots will keep socks and ankles dry. These need
not be expensive climbing or rambling boots of high quality and
price – inexpensive rubber-soled "fell boots" sold at most outdoor
shops for a few pounds are perfectly adequate, whilst early and
late in the year, especially when there is snow about, or whenever
it is very wet, the humble wellington is as good as anything for
shorter distances, especially with an extra thick sock in it.

Rainwear, is, alas, usually essential. An old gabardine raincoat,
nylon or plastic mac or waterproof anorak is again adequate if you
do not plan to go too far; but a longer, heavy nylon cagoule is
invaluable if you intend to stay out in the wet for any time.

For all but the shortest distances a rucksack is essential. This
need not be the towering variety beloved of the younger generation anxious to give an image of the Himalayas, but might well be
a simple nylon or canvas day-sack, capable of holding water-
proofs, gloves, a little food and other essentials in a way which
keeps both your hands free. If you have more to carry, however, a
framed rucksack is very much more comfortable. Nothing is more

irritating than hand or shoulder baggage which can be seriously in the way when trying to cross a stile.

Once you leave the valley floor life gets a shade more complex. On the higher slopes and upland pastures in the Dales – what I will call the uplands – expect magnificent walking, superb views and a good deal more wind and weather. Once you begin to climb in the Dales you cannot compromise. A decent windproof anorak and a pair of strong boots really are essential and whilst traditionally minded ladies and Scotsmen may disagree, warm wool trousers or breeches are equally necessary. Jeans are not recommended because of their inability to retain heat when wet. As well as a cagoule, overtrousers are highly recommended; not only will they save vulnerable parts of the body getting cold and wet, but in emergencies and sudden cold conditions they can help you keep warm. Always fill the rucksack with supplies of food for your anticipated requirements together with emergency rations in case of delay – chocolate can be a life-saver. Though you can usually find supplies of pure water in the Dales (a general rule is to see if the stream comes down from any human habitation – if not, it is likely to be safe if it is running swiftly), it is better to carry adequate supplies of liquid, and in all seasons carry an extra sweater, gloves, scarf and a warm woolly hat – more heat loss occurs through the head than any part of the body. It is always wise to plan for an unexpected delay on the hills when extra clothing may be required, or for a sudden change in the weather when the temperature may drop dramatically.

Take a simple first-aid kit with you – sticking plasters, a couple of bandages, lint and safety-pins are enough to cope with most simple emergencies.

In the real highlands, moor tops, mountains or the high fell, you must treat the hills with even more respect. The tops can provide some of the worst conditions known in Britain, biting sub-zero temperatures and sub-Arctic conditions, where deaths from exposure can and do occur to the foolhardy and ill-equipped. There are remarkable differences of temperature in only a few hundred feet, and it can be mild in the valley and deathly cold on a hillside. I have walked the Pennine ridges in June clad in only a shirt and shorts, but taken care to have woollies with me; of course you can have hot, windless days when full mountain gear would be pedantry, but there are also

deceptive spring and autumn days when sudden storms or fogs can turn a pleasant afternoon into a nightmare, when very survival depends on fell craft. The safe rule is never to go ill-equipped into the hills, nor to go beyond the limits of your strength and experience. Fell craft is the art of understanding the country you are in and its climate, and knowing your own capacity and remaining well within it. Always carry a compass with you, and learn how to use it; examine your escape routes and, if conditions or circumstances change, know how to reach them. Learn to navigate by the shape of a fell, dry-stone walls, obvious landmarks such as farms, roads, copses – though remember woodland may have been planted or felled since the map you are using was printed. You may rarely have to use that compass, but when you do it could save your life.

It is always good sense to leave word with someone before you go out, in case of accident – and should you change your plan and not return, to let them know. It is also sensible to walk in the wildest places with one or more companions; though, having said that, solitary hill walking is one of life's true joys. If you do walk alone in the hills, do so in the full knowledge of the risks involved.

If things do get difficult, a few basic strategies can ensure survival. The real killer on hills is hypothermia – exposure, caused by a combination of tiredness and cold. Its symptoms are a lack of co-ordination and a slurring of speech. Walking too far on too little food is one cause; at the first sign in yourself or a companion get off the tops as quickly as possible, or if it is too far to do so safely, rest in the shelter of a wall, take food and, if necessary, seek help. A polythene survival bag can be bought at most outdoor shops cheaply – in case of accident on the tops it can keep victims warm a few extra, precious hours whilst help comes. The crucial need is to keep body temperature up with maximum clothing and whatever shelter is available, with a healthy person acting as a human blanket to the injured or suffering person whilst a third companion makes for the nearest human habitation to raise the alarm. A 999 call will automatically bring out Fell Rescue services in the Dales.

Fell Rescue in the Pennines is an entirely voluntary matter, though the Dales teams work closely with the police and ambulance services in the area. There are four teams in the Dales – the

Upper Wharfedale Fell Rescue Association in Grassington, the Cave Rescue Organization at Clapham, the Swaledale Fell Rescue based at Reeth, and the Sedbergh Fell Rescue based at Sedbergh. These teams of local people – farmers, quarry workers, mechanics, shopkeepers, teachers – have detailed knowledge of the area and can reach the site of an incident at amazing speed. They are the fell walkers' finest insurance. You can help them in two ways. First of all by staying out of trouble, by avoiding any foolish, rash or thoughtless action which will require them giving their time and effort on your behalf. You can also help them when you are in the Dales by the simple expedient of making a donation, either in one of the collecting-boxes in most pubs, shops and cafés, or by post to the National Park Officer, Grassington, near Skipton, North Yorkshire (cheques payable to North Yorkshire County Council) who will ensure the donation is shared between the four teams.

Enough of such sombre thoughts. For the vast majority of people, for the vast majority of the time, the Dales present few such hazards. Your main concern will, in fact, be path finding, and for this decent maps are essential. No guidebook can adequately replace a decent Ordnance Survey map.

My own experience with the new 1:50,000 Ordnance Survey maps is that they are adequate in areas where paths are well used and easy to find – in some parts of the Yorkshire Dales – but nothing like as informative or easy to use as the 1:25,000 scale. The National Park area is fortunate in that there are two 1:25,000 Outdoor Leisure Series maps, The Three Peaks and Malham and Upper Wharfedale, which are of enormous value, detailing as they do public footpaths and field walls with great clarity. The Dales are equally fortunate to have a footpath map-maker of great talent at work in the region – Arthur Gemmell of Otley whose Stile Maps are excellent aids for the walker, interpreting the local footpath system in a way that is especially helpful to the rambler. Stile maps currently exist for the Bolton Abbey, Grassington, Malham, Aysgarth, Three Peaks, Sedbergh (Howgills) and Sedbergh (South) districts, whilst Ralph Bradley has produced a Stile map for Hawes. These are available from most local bookshops or by post – prices on request from Stile Maps, Mercury House, Otley, West Yorkshire.

Not everyone understands exactly what a footpath is. A footpath is not so much a physical thing, a track on the ground, as a public right of way, that is the right of passage across private ground. In theory, at least, a path has a specified width – it may be one metre or perhaps two, so that a walker crossing a field should in practice keep to that single strip of land and not, with his companions, spread four of five abreast, especially if the land is long meadow-grass, and vulnerable to wear and damage.

A footpath has, as its name implies, rights of foot only, which means you cannot ride a bike or a horse along it. You can take a dog along it, providing that dog is under control, either on a lead or to heel.

A bridleway on the other hand has rights of foot and bridle rights which means you can walk or ride on a pedal cycle or on horseback along it. It is assumed that cyclists will yield to pedestrians on such a route.

There are other kinds of rights along some old ways and tracks; these may include droving rights (the rights to drive pigs or sheep along) or vehicular rights, which means that it is legally possible to drive a motorbike or car along the way. Many green lanes with vehicular rights are county roads, others are not maintained by the county council.

Footpaths and bridleways are clearly shown on the newer Ordnance Survey maps as red dots and dashes respectively on the 1:50,000 Landranger maps and as green dots and dashes on the Outdoor Leisure and Second Series 1:25,000 maps. Note that the old First Series 1:25,000 maps (blue covers) do not show rights of way, and footpaths indicated on these maps are therefore unreliable unless used in conjunction with a 1:50,000 map which will help confirm which paths are or are not public. It should be pointed out, too, that all maps show black dotted lines marked FP which simply indicate the line of a path on the ground, but which may not be a right of way, and in using it (there are several examples in the Dales) you could cause nuisance. If in doubt keep to the green or red dots.

A further complication lies in the fact that most of the county roads mentioned above are not in fact indicated on the Ordnance maps except as white roads and it is very difficult to tell which are public and which are not. In fact most enclosed moorland tracks in the Dales are public, and indeed you may have to share some of them with the occasional trail-riding motor cyclist who has as much legal right to be there as the walker. But the existence of a white road on the map is no guarantee of its public status.

This is why the kind of map produced especially for walkers in the Dales, such as those produced by Arthur Gemmell for Stile are especially useful, showing the official rights of way as shown on the County Council Definitive Map as well as county roads and other routes normally open for the walker that can be used without fear of trespass or disturbance.

Having spoken about rights, it is also wise to speak of responsibilities. You will be always welcomed in the Dales by Dales farmers if you treat their property with respect and consider their needs. I have mentioned already the need to walk in single file across meadowland in late spring and early summer so as not to damage that hay crop so essential for them to ensure economic survival, through the long Pennine winters. Close gates behind you, unless they are clearly propped open for some purpose. Unless you absolutely have to, never climb a dry-stone wall; this weakens its structure, and if it falls, you not only risk serious injury but a heavy maintenance bill for the farmer and, if stock stray, hours wasted in recovering them. Do not leave litter of any kind; sheep can choke on plastic, or be injured by glass. Stones scattered in a meadow can smash a mowing-machine blade. Above all, uncontrolled dogs at lambing time are a nightmare for the farmer, causing loss of life among new-born stock or abortions among pregnant ewes. Even the most friendly and well-behaved pet can alarm a flock of sheep; farmers would always feel less nervous if, in those critical months of March and April, dogs might be left at home.

Never touch or attempt to pick up a new-born lamb; your action could separate mother and lamb with fatal consequences. Should you find what you believe to be a sick or injured animal, report the matter to the farm rather than take action yourself.

Open country is always a slightly sensitive area with farmers. In some areas walkers have traditionally wandered at will, in others, especially on grouse moors, gamekeepers and landowners resent the presence of walkers at almost any time of the year. The most certain counsel is to keep to rights of way unless you can be certain that *de facto* access, as it is known, exists, or, as around Bolton Abbey and Barden, the moors are open to the public under the terms of a special access agreement with the county council.

The important thing is less the legalities of the countryside and more the courtesies. Farmers resent nothing more deeply than the kind of people who, on someone else's land, demand "rights". A pleasant word to a farmer when you cross his land makes him feel you do not just take him for granted; he will often readily give permission to go where no legal right of way exists but resents it if he finds you trespassing. Of course there are the irascible ones, just as there are unreasonable members of any group, ramblers included. But in the main they are, in the Dales, long-suffering and surprisingly tolerant, and your consideration and courtesy is the least they deserve.

Paths are not difficult to find in the Dales. The ancient tracks and green roads are usually obvious enough, especially when enclosed within a long sweep of dry-stone wall. Other footpaths are usually indicated by stone step or gap stiles, and in recent years by the National Park ladder or "A" stiles which make clearly visible waymarks on upland and felltop paths. Where signposting and waymarking has occurred (yellow arrows for footpaths, blue for bridleways) path finding is easy; more often, however, it is a question of careful map-reading, orientating yourself from the field walls especially, looking for the stiles. With experience you begin to develop an instinct for a footpath, nosing them out where they follow a natural logic through a field or along a hillside, usually (though not always) following the contours or shape of the land. Footpaths do not appear by magic – they respond to needs, and, even if the needs have changed, the paths are still discernible to the trained eye, if not immediately visible on the ground – between farms, to avoid floods, to the church (and pub). Nosing out an old path is a joy all of itself.

If you find a path that is seriously blocked (and I do not just mean a "lambing stone" or old can lodged in a gap-stile to prevent young lambs escaping), you are legally entitled to continue your way by any convenient means possible until you can rejoin the footpath; which may not be particularly convenient to you, but please avoid causing any damage – this will not help improve relationships in the future. Alternatively you can simply remove the obstruction and proceed, and whilst I have some sympathy for the kind of ramblers who carry large German wire-cutters in the pocket of their rucksack, such commando tactics are not normally necessary in the Yorkshire Dales. Better to simply report the obstruction to the relevant local authority and let the warden or footpath officer sort the problem out with the farmer, who probably has just forgotten about the path anyhow, but will not forget the fact if a damaged fence allows the cattle to get in the hay. If the blockage is in the National Park write to The National Park Officer, Hebden Road, Grassington, Skipton, North Yorkshire; outside the park if you are in North Yorkshire write to the County Surveyor, County Hall, Northallerton; in south Lakeland, Eden or Bradford Metropolitan District Council areas, the appropriate authority is the Surveyor or Engineer, the Town Hall, Kendal, Penrith or Bradford respectively. The complaint will arrive on the right desk eventually. In your letter state where the blockage is (grid reference please) the date you discovered it, and what it consists of (barbed-wire, old corrugated iron etc.) so that the officer concerned will know what to look for.

Bulls should be treated in a similar manner. Changes in legislation make non-dairy bulls with cows legal. My advice is to treat any bull with or without cows with the utmost caution. If the bull is far enough away, and peaceful enough, see where the path runs, where an escape route lies, and forget the bull is there. Do not look at it, or rush past it; ignore it and it will ignore you. If, on the other hand, it is close, looking frisky, or there is no decent escape route, or you are not very agile, or you have young children with you, give him a wide berth – and report the incident to the local police station if you think the law is being broken. To be fair, life can be difficult for Dales farmers, especially on those huge upland enclosures where there may literally be nowhere else to put the bull. Do not trust bulls – but frankly I find more problems caused by frisky horses whose flying hooves can be lethal, or even, on one unforgettable occasion, by a charging pig.

Which leads neatly to the question of walking-sticks. Most walkers, in England at least, seem to regard use of a walking-stick as a sign of incipient senility. I disagree. I confess to being a walking-stick man. The genuine Alpinist will, in fact, go for the shoulder-height stick or staff, which is useful in many tricky conditions. I compromise with a standard crooked ash stick which is invaluable for short slippery slopes, mud, mire, getting under or over barbed-wire or electric fences (get a companion to hook up the wire), testing the depth of bog or deep becks before you put your boot in, lashing back nettles, thistles and things that inhabit overgrown lanes, and above all beasts. You can keep almost anything with horns or teeth at bay for a few precious seconds with a walking-stick, and a well-swung stick can turn a vicious dog into a whimpering cur with a flick of the wrist.

It can, moreover, be a useful companion on a longer walk, helping you to build up the rhythm of a mile-devouring pace.

I would not be without a walking-stick.

Most walkers coming to the Dales these days come by car. Where possible please leave the vehicle in one of the official car parks in the Dales rather than blocking a village green or market place for the day. If you do leave it by a verge, make sure that you are not causing an obstruction, whether to traffic coming up and down the lane, (delivery vehicles and lorries often have to use narrow Dales lanes and tracks) or to tractors or cattle wanting to enter a field. Nothing is more irritating to a farmer than if he cannot move his stock because a thoughtless motorist has blocked his gate whilst he wanders the fells, or for that matter to a householder in a Dales village who cannot get his car out on a Sunday afternoon because his drive or gateway is blocked.

A word of warning about keeping your car locked. Car thieves have increased dramatically in number and in activity in recent years during the tourist season and it pays not only to make sure your car is locked before you leave it, but to ensure any irreplaceable valuables, including keys, licences and cheque cards are taken with you.

Remember it is illegal to take a motor vehicle onto open moorland along a footpath or bridleway or into a private field; by so doing you could be committing a criminal offence.

Public transport is still remarkably good in the Yorkshire Dales, and it is perfectly possible to have an excellent day's walking relying on trains and buses, especially from West Yorkshire, or to get around the area using scheduled bus and train services. Local timetables are displayed at bus stations and information offices, and comprehensive local timetables are available. Of particular value to the rambler is *Dales Wayfarer*, an unlimited travel ticket which is valid on the entire West Yorkshire rail and bus network to Skipton, Settle, Giggleswick, Harrogate and Knaresborough by rail, and then on scheduled buses as far as Buckden, Grassington, Bolton Abbey, Hawes, Pateley Bridge, Ripon, Brimham

Rocks and Fountains Abbey. Leaflets are available from bus and rail stations or by post from West Yorkshire PTE, Metro House, West Parade, Wakefield, West Yorkshire.

The Dayrider unlimited travel ticket is available on West Yorkshire RCC (National) red buses covering an area from Leeds, Harrogate, York and Bradford into Wharfedale and Nidderdale, whilst the United Explorer ticket permits travel from Teesside, Ripon and Richmond on United bus services through Wensleydale and Swaledale. All these facilities operate in the opposite direction, that is you can buy a ticket on a bus in the Dales for a trip into the nearby town or city, an invaluable facility if you are staying in the Dales and a torrential downpour makes walking impossible.

There is much to be said, in fact, for combining the flexibility of the car with the convenience of the bus. Many superb walks can be planned and executed by the discerning walker who is prepared to leave his car at an appropriate car park, catch the bus to an outward point and then return on foot with all afternoon or all day available for it. The motorist who is prepared to do this can, like the public transport users, escape from the tyranny of the car that insists you return to the point you started from. One of the joys, indeed glories, of the Dales is that you can start a walk in one valley and cross the watershed to the next; what a bore to climb back into the original valley if you have the alternative of a bus or a train to bring you back from the other side of the ridge; how much more satisfying to climb to a dale head, cross the high fell and descend into a different world beyond.

The best recreational transport service of all in the Dales is, of course, Dales Rail, but I leave that for a later chapter.

Finally, it will be noted that even when suggesting specific walks I rarely mention either distances or time in the text. This is because, in an area like the Dales "distance" is a relative term when walking – five miles over rough country can be longer than fifteen along easy paths and lanes. Distances can be misleading. Perhaps the continental measurement in time is a better one, (a route estimated at "an hour" makes some allowance for terrain). You can, with experience, compare the average speed implied on an Alpine signpost with your own. But I have chosen to avoid giving either distances or times to force the reader to use a good field guide or map. Intelligent map-reading, intepretation of contours and other features, is the only reliable method of estimating a walk's likely demands, and even then you must allow yourself a generous margin of error.

REFERENCE

Pathfinder – Navigation and safety in the Hills, Kenneth Oldham (Dalesman, 1980)

The law of Footpaths, Ian Campbell (Commons Society, 1979)

Tackle Rambling, Alan Mattingly (Stanley Paul, 1981)

Rights of Way: A Guide to Law and Practice, Paul Clayden and John Trevelyan (Open Spaces Society, Ramblers Association 1983)

Information on bus services in the Dales can be obtained from:

West Yorkshire Road Car Co., PO Box 24, Harrogate, North Yorkshire. Tel. 66061. (Wharfedale, Nidderdale)

United Automobile Co., Feethams, Darlington, Co. Durham. Tel. 68771. (Wensleydale, Swaledale)

Ribble Motors, Blackhall Road, Kendal, Cumbria. Tel. 20932. (Western Dales)

4

Wharfedale

There cannot be many rivers in England with their own Roman goddess; an altar found in Ilkley refers to Verbeia, goddess of the Wharfe.

Whoever Verbeia was, she must have been a beautiful goddess, for the Wharfe is a beautiful river, the most beautiful river in England many would say, and who am I to contradict such received wisdom?

Perhaps the lady was a wicked temptress because the Wharfe, for all its seductive loveliness, is a treacherous, fierce river, with vicious currents and a propensity to rise quickly. More people drown in the Wharfe than any other river in Yorkshire. Choose your bathing spots with care.

Be that as it may, the divinity of the Wharfe must lie in the countryside through which it passes. Of all the Dales, Wharfedale is the most romantic, with a heady voluptuous beauty which is attractive in all seasons, but perhaps never more so than in the bright light of spring with snow still on the high tops and long limestone terraces, or again, in autumn, when the colour of the woodlands around Bolton Abbey and Barden is one of the glories of England.

You can, of course, simply follow the riverside of the Wharfe for much of its length, in the Dales almost continuously from Ilkley to Cam Fell, its source. It is this that forms the marvellous first part of the Dales Way, the eighty-one mile long footpath from Ilkley to Windermere that is described in a later part of this book. But not even the Dales Way can do full justice to the superb variety of walking that Wharfedale offers, in truth right down the Lower Dale to its confluence with the Ouse at Cawood below Tadcaster. For simplicity I shall divide the dale into three principal sections within our area – Mid-Wharfedale which is from Ilkley

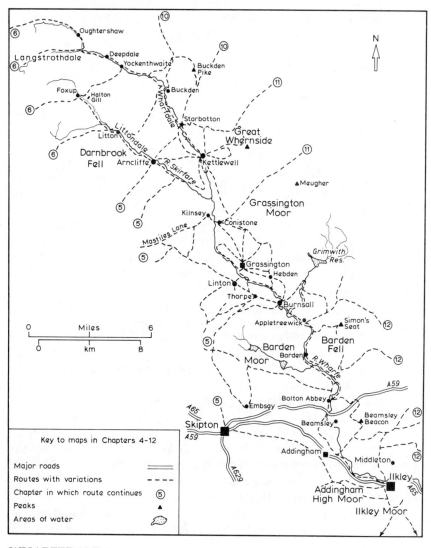

WHARFEDALE

to Burnsall; Upper Wharfedale from Burnsall to Buckden, and Littondale and Langstrothdale which includes the major tributary of the Wharfe, the Skirfare, and the most mountainous part of the river as it descends from the wild fell country as little more than a mountain beck through Langstrothdale.

Mid-Wharfedale

Ilkley has long been a favourite focal point for ramblers. Two reasons for this are that the trains and the buses all went there from the towns of West Riding, and the Dales countryside and Ilkley Moor in particular seem to descend right into the town centre. It is, in a very real sense, the place where urban West Yorkshire ends and the real Dales country begins, a frontier town whose solid, well-built houses reflect all the virtues of hard work and thrift of the Yorkshire wool trade that financed them. But beyond, in the Dales, romance and freedom begin.

You can get on to the moor by walking up the main street, Brook Street, continuing by the little park that surrounds the brook in question, and following the road up to the moor edge. If you are a little lazy you can even take your car up there, and leave it in the car park by the moor edge.

Ilkley Moor, being an urban common, offers the walker complete freedom to wander anywhere across its heather, bilberry, rough grass and bracken. A maze of paths gives credence to the number of adherents to Yorkshire's most illustrious song. Whether or not "'baht 'at'', walkers have given planners some problems with erosion by feet, with tracks and paths taking quite a scuffing and hammering from foot and hoof.

But it is still a splendid place to walk. If you have never walked on Ilkley Moor before, start with the path straight to the little white cottage directly ahead, White Wells. You will soon pick up some steps, remnants of a donkey path where, in the eighteenth century rheumatic gentlemen and portly ladies were carried up to take the ice-cold waters of the little spa.

White Wells has, in fact, been beautifully restored, and a small interpretive display tells the story of the little spring and health baths.

From White Wells follow the path that contours east, below Ilkley Crags and past the tarns, through a pinewood shelter belt to the Cow and Calf rocks, another sacred shrine of rambling history where many a passionate rally for the rights of the ordinary man to walk upon the hills has been held, under the shadow of the great gritstone crag and single huge boulder that give the name to the landmark.

Most people who park their cars here and wander across to the old quarry to see young climbers cutting their teeth on the nursery slopes, sit in the cars to enjoy the view and read the *News of the World* or wander across to the pub, have little idea of the passionate outpourings in the 1930s and later, when working-class ramblers from the mill towns of Yorkshire kept from the grouse moors by keepers and their dogs, met to fight for their rights.

Such battles belong, be it hoped, to an angry and intolerant past. Most people will enjoy the splendid panoramic view from these edges across the crowded, busy part of the Wharfe Valley, looking across towards Otley, The Chevin and Washburndale, or downriver to the gritstone hummock Almscliffe Crag.

You can, of course, follow another hallowed route more or less due south from White Wells up past the Twelve Apostles, a ring of stones dating from Bronze Age times and full of evocative power to this day; one of many prehistoric fragments on this moor. The track continues over Rombalds Moor – the name given to the whole massif that includes Ilkley Moor – to become a paved pack-horse way to Dick Hudson's pub in Airedale.

But our concern is strictly with the true high Dales country, westwards. For a splendid walk along the moorland edge, leave the moor road below White Wells to follow a track which soon becomes a path, above the wooded Heber's Ghyll to pass the Swastika Stone, now enclosed in a small fenced compound, a strange rock carving of the ancient Indo-European good-luck symbol, again a kind of Bronze Age wayside shrine, for the path you follow is part of an ancient trans-Pennine trade route through the Aire Gap and into Wharfedale, heading for the plains of York at the eastern seaboard.

Continue on the path along the edge of Addingham High Moor to where an obvious path descends; this leads to a lower path returning pleasantly back into Ilkley by Briery Wood Farm and Heber's Ghyll, and some splendid Edwardian villas; or you can continue to Windgate Nick, a steep and narrow nick in the rock, perhaps natural, perhaps man-made (such artificial "nicks" were used by Iron Age man as waymarks) leading to the Doubler Stones, wind-carved pillars of rocks forming strange features above the otherwise featureless moorland.

Or a choice of pleasant footpath routes is available into Addingham (frequent buses along the main road back into Ilkley) from where there are plenty of opportunities for some attractive circular walks on the north side of the Wharfe back to Ilkley. The really historically minded might, however, like to trace this old pass through the Pennines by picking up the track at the north-west extremity of Addingham which follows the line of the Roman road over Draughton Moor, High Edge and Skipton Moor into Skipton, again a fine and dramatic walk.

But the country north of Ilkley should not be neglected. Once across Ilkley Bridge (really the new bridge as Ilkley Bridge is the old pack-horse bridge three hundred metres upstream) a number of routes, the most popular being "Catholic Gate" past the retreat at Tivoli, lead up to Middleton Moor, where for the energetic splendid ancient tracks cross over the high moorland towards Washburndale, none more famous than the old corn-dealers' path, known as "Badger Gate" that runs up from Beamsley along Wards End and Longridge heading for Timble and Knaresborough. Badgers were corn-dealers – this was once a busy route; it now requires careful path finding over wild and almost featureless moorland. The Roman road, marked on the Ordnance maps, crosses this way, but is now almost indecipherable over the peaty moorland.

The jewel of these moors is undoubtedly Beamsley Beacon, a strange peaked hill, almost volcanic in appearance, that dominates the countryside for miles around.

Climbing Beamsley Beacon is a wonderful experience. You can of course cheat and take your car to the roadside above Langbar and walk the final eight hundred metres to the summit. Far better to have traced your way up by footpaths from Ilkley, or alternatively from Addingham where a path crosses the river at the suspension bridge by West Hall and climbs either along an ancient, fascinating medieval lane known as Langbar Lane (often overgrown in late summer) or a parallel field path to the southeast via Leyfield which is almost equally attractive.

Beamsley Beacon is strictly the name of the ancient beacon on Howber Hill, one of that chain of beacons which crossed the north of England whereby, you recall, news of impending disasters such as the Spanish Armada, could be transmitted by bonfires lit in quick succession on the highest hills.

It is, in truth, a splendid little mountain, with a viewpoint that totally belies its relatively modest height, commanding as it does panoramic views of Wharfedale and Rombald's Moor. The summit is, by virtue of an old deed, open access land where you can wander at will during the hours of daylight; the limitation against the hours of darkness hardly seems necessary as few but the most masochistic would wander on the beacon in hours of darkness. Perhaps the Victorian worthies who granted the summit of Howber Hill to the people, secretly feared Chartist meetings by torchlight or even by light of a beacon as subversive rebellion stalked the land.

Law-abiding citizens and ramblers are more likely to climb its upturned ark of a peak when there is a view to enjoy, and the best way of all is to approach it from the east or the north, where the view comes suddenly and dramatically as a splendid surprise. It is a murderously steep climb from Ling Chapel, but a glorious moment when you finally get there; this route can be reached from Kex Gill Beck and Deerstones, or equally from the green lane from Hazel Wood past Howgill Farm.

A classic walk from Addingham (convenient car park by the Memorial Hall – frequent buses from Leeds, Ilkley, Skipton and Keighley) is to follow the lane that leads north-westwards out of Addingham, past the new primary school, past Highfield House and Highfield Farm, turning northwards along the side of the ridge (superb views behind and across to Beamsley Beacon) towards Lob Wood. Here the path descends through pasture with a glorious view up Wharfedale past Bolton Bridge, into Lob Wood, under the old railway viaduct and along the B6160, soon branching off to the riverside path to Bolton Bridge and on to Bolton Abbey. The return route is across the stepping-stones or wooden foot-bridge, following the little enclosed bridleway which soon branches off the main woodland path, uphill to Storiths, turning south across the fields (waymarked) to New Hall Farm and the main A59 road at the lovely Beamsley Hospital – charming seventeenth-century almshouses built around a circular chapel, and erected by the great Lady Anne Clifford of Skipton Castle. The path now descends to Kex Gill which can be followed to Deerstones and the thrilling ascent of the beacon past Ling Chapel, and a choice of routes back across the suspension bridge to Addingham.

Bolton Abbey is an ideal starting-point for anyone walking in Wharfedale, and the priory's perfect romantic setting by the Wharfe must make it one of the most beautiful ruins in England. The word "ruin" must be carefully qualified because the priory church remains intact to serve as the parish church for the local community, and the whole complex of medieval ruins and church, the gatehouses converted in eighteenth-century Gothic taste into a shooting-lodge, and the old school now the vicarage, adds to the feeling of continuity.

Naturally at summer weekends and whenever the sun shines, Bolton Abbey is thronged with visitors. Leeds and Bradford are, after all, only an hour away by car, with direct bus services at weekends, and why stay in Leeds or Bradford on a sunny afternoon if you could be at Bolton Abbey? Yet the priory and its parkland and woodland, which are part of the Duke of Devonshire's Chatsworth Estates in Yorkshire, absorb this huge pressure of visitors with astonishing ease. You can leave your car in the car park at the top of the village, stroll through the famous "hole in the wall", enjoy the abbey ruins, and return in time for afternoon tea at the Post Office tea gardens. More ambitiously you can cross the wooden bridge by the stepping-stones noting the little waterfall on the right painted by Turner and drawn by Ruskin, and with little more than a couple of hours to spare, take the riverside or higher woodland path (the latter has the better views) and wander through the carefully landscaped paths to the ford across Pickles Gill (foot-bridge for walkers) and along the riverside crossing to find an excellent cup of tea, hot or cold snack, or full meal – at almost any time of the year – at the Cavendish Pavilion. Return by the riverside to the Cavendish Fountain (erected to the memory of Lord Frederick Cavendish, diplomat, who was assassinated in Phoenix Park, Dublin, in 1882) and the village car park.

Or you can continue through Strid Wood Nature Trail, along more splendidly laid out pathways at various levels through the wood, which were, in fact, the creation early last century of the excellent Reverend William Carr, Vicar of Bolton, whose other claim to fame was the production of the first dictionary of Craven dialect and the breeding of the celebrated Craven heifer, a huge heifer that gazes down from many a local pub sign.

The trails, for which a small entrance charge is made, are interpreted by an informative and well-illustrated booklet and map which highlights all the various viewpoints and "seats" so beloved of Victorian topographers. The woods, mainly natural oak-woods, are a rich habitat of wildlife, especially bird life. But the real highlight of Strid Woods is inevitably the Strid itself, the notorious channel through water-carved gritstone, through which the full weight and force of the Wharfe rushes, carving lethal underground chambers in which many a drowning has occurred, being caused most often, one is told, by people taking an ill-fated leap across the Strid and perishing in the powerful currents. It is, inevitably, a place of folk tales and legend, from the Boy of Egremond celebrated in ballads to lugubrious tales of attempted murders in more recent days. But the real quality of the woods is their quite overpowering natural beauty, breathtaking in any season but most of all in late October or early November when they are afire with crimson, orange, gold and copper.

The Strid Wood paths converge, beyond the High Strid, on a rocky riverside path that finally relaxes into open riverside country past the old Bradford Corporation Aqueduct to the lovely seventeenth-century bridge at Barden.

Just above the bridge is Barden Tower, hunting-lodge of the Clifford family, Plantagenet lords of Skipton Castle, most notably the Shepherd Lord, Henry, tenth Lord Clifford (1453-1523) brought up in exile, in the house of a Cumbrian shepherd during the Wars of the Roses, eventually inheriting his estates as the Lancastrian fortunes were restored and living in the peaceful surroundings of Barden as a scholar – though he was later to fight at Flodden. Wordsworth recalls his life with suitable picturesque and patriotic colouring in his poem "Song at the Feast of Brougham Castle" in 1807.

You can return on a path along the far bank of the river, a walk every bit as attractive, to Cavendish Pavilion.

The Cavendish (ample car parking – small charge – nearby) is the starting-point of another justly famous Dales walk, Simon Seat. The route follows the far side of the river up to Waterfall Cottage, crossing the Old Park with its huge, mournful ancient oaks, and a grove of saplings planted in 1980 to mark the fiftieth anniversary of the West Riding Ramblers' Association – a fitting tribute to the new spirit of mutual respect and trust between ramblers and landowners – to Posforth Gill.

This path leads through the Valley of Desolation, so-called because of a terrible landslip in the middle of last century which wrecked the woods, emerging at a gate above the plantation and on to the open moor of Barden Fell. This entire area is part of the Barden Fell and Barden Moor Access Area, an agreement by which the famous grouse moors and surroundings areas are open to the public throughout the year, except for days on which shooting takes place or during times of high fire risk when they can be closed by order of the Ministry of Agriculture. The moorlands are subject to certain by-laws, most of which are perfectly sensible and natural for ramblers (copies are posted at the main entrance points) with the exception of one which insists that no dogs, with or without lead, are allowed on the access areas. This may upset dog lovers, but the rule is part of the agreement to achieve a reasonable compromise between the needs of game conservation and access by the public, and must be respected.

The track to Simon Seat is clear and well defined, crossing Great Aygill Beck past a splendid stone table – presumably the site of extravagant Victorian picnics – on to the craggy and rocky summit of Simon Seat, not high at 1,550 feet (485 metres) but a magnificent viewpoint looking over into Skyreholme, a tributary valley of the Wharfe, and along the main dale to Burnsall. At weekends in spring and summer you are likely to meet one of the Yorkshire Dales National Park voluntary wardens on duty around the summit, keeping an eye on visitors to ensure by-laws are being obeyed, but more positively to offer help and advice, which often includes a considerable knowledge of natural history, to anyone with time to chat.

The descent is either directly down the zigzagging path through the heather to Dalehead and either along Howgill Lane or to High Skyreholme, or to the south-west along another cairned track descending below Earl Seat, through the woodlands to Howgill. From Howgill the riverside path leads past Drebley Steps back to Barden, the Cavendish Pavilion and Bolton Abbey. Should you decide to cross Drebley Steps by the by, remember that apart from to Drebley itself no right of way exists along the west bank of the river, and your presence will cause disturbance.

The whole of Barden Fell is available to the wanderer, but apart from one or two notable routes, including the Dales Way Harrogate link over Long Ridge and Rocking Stone, described in the Washburndale section of this book, and the old green lane from Skyreholme over Pockstones Moor, much of it is a rather dreary and characterless waste, not without its dangers in the Pockstones area where former army artillery ranges have left the occasional corroding and unexploded shell lying on the moor, which in recent times has caused at least one terrible fatal accident. Should you find any suspicious objects in this area, leave well alone and report them to the police at the first opportunity.

Barden Moor on the other side of the Wharfe is altogether different, an area of moorland of enormous interest and character, a superb heather moorland offering a true sense of wilderness and yet dramatic views into the rich and fertile valleys below. It is, for me, an area of changing moods, often sombre, sometimes benign, always full of character, as if, like Thomas Hardy's Egdon Heath, it has a spirit and a being of its own.

It is, conveniently, crossed by a public bridleway from Bolton Abbey, a track which begins on the main road near Bolton Hall, winds through West Bank Wood, and, marked by posts, climbs to Middle Hare Head and Halton Height where it crosses the Embsay road, before entering the moor itself, climbing high above the two reservoirs and along Brown Bank to emerge, with a fitting sense of climax, high above Rylstone, not far south of Rylstone Cross. This important and ancient bridleway (allegedly the route taken by Emily Norton and the White Doe in the legendary *White Doe of Rylstone* tale) has useful connecting links from Halton East, Embsay and Eastby, and, as a public right of way remains open in the shooting season and for well-controlled dogs.

A variety of walks can be planned on and around the moor. An interesting circular walk can be planned following the track and path to Upper Barden Reservoir, returning along the reservoir track (cars can be parked at Halton Heights or near Barden Scale) or by continuing along Gill Beck Head to leave the moor at one of the official access points to Burnsall or Thorpe, or even by following the edge of the moor round right up to the dizzy heights of Cracoe War Memorial and Rylstone Cross. This is all magnificent full-blooded fell walking, requiring the rambler to cross some pretty wild and tough country, not, indeed to everyone's taste. But for anyone who loves the wild places, seeks solitude and, on occasions, some spectacular wildlife, Barden Moor has much to offer, and for that reason is highly regarded by experienced fell walkers.

Notices are posted at official entry points on days when Barden Fell or Barden Moor are closed to the public for shooting or because of fire risk; shooting begins on 12 August and runs to the end of the year, and never takes place on Sundays. If in doubt a phone call to the National Park Office, Grassington 752748, will confirm if the access areas are open.

Those people who, for a variety of reasons, resent the shooting of grouse on the fell and moor, should also appreciate that, as elsewhere in northern Britain, the sport provides the justification for game and wildlife conservation, and heather moorland management. The superb purple of our Yorkshire heather moors are, in effect, an artificial habitat preserved because grouse shooting is a profitable use of the land. The grouse that are culled in the autumn would in any event perish on overstocked moors in the winter. The rambler who loves the freedom of the fells has, in effect, no better ally than the sportsman, for, if grouse shooting ceased, within a decade most of our magnificent moors would be fenced and ploughed out of existence as grassland improvement or planted with conifers.

But to return to the dale. Although there are many excellent footpaths in the Appletreewick area, parking is a little limited, and Burnsall is, in many respects, a more obvious and convenient centre, a beautifully situated and historic village, with a decent car park, overflowing onto the far side of the river at busy times, and with good facilities.

One obvious and popular walk is to go, indeed, down river via Woodhouse Farm to Appletreewick, an attractive linear village with one or two medieval buildings, following field paths to Skyreholme, then along the lane to Parceval Hall (delightful gardens open during the summer months) and into Trollers' Gill.

Trollers' Gill is an example of a narrow limestone gorge, carved out by forces far more terrifying than the present modest beck, rich in atmosphere and craggy splendour. The path bears left past old mines climbing out of the gill and continues to Fancarl on the Pateley Bridge road. Bear due west along the path that climbs over moorland by Hell Hole and pick up a bridleway across Appletreewick pasture. This crosses to Kail Lane, a green track around that strange limestone reef knoll, Kail Hill. The track emerges on the Burnsall road just opposite Woodhouse Farm, for Burnsall.

Another popular walk of around seven miles is to take the path on the far side of the river from Burnsall, climbing uphill (waymarked) across the road to Hebden towards Raikes House, and then along the field path by the side of Langerton Hill to Dibble's bridge, returning on a lovely valleyside path along the far side of Barden Beck to Hartlington and Burnsall.

But from Burnsall few people will resist the temptation to follow the path upstream behind the Red Lion to Loup Scar, for Hebden, Grassington and Linton. This leads us, with a neat inevitability, into Upper Wharfedale.

Upper Wharfedale
Grassington must undoubtedly be one of the very best centres for rambling in the Dales. It is perfectly situated to permit easy access to every part of Wharfedale and makes an ideal central point for a longer stay walking holiday, offering every type of accommodation from three-star hotel to modest guest-house and self-catering cottages and flats, with caravan and campsites in the vicinity. Whilst being still a working village, it takes itself seriously as a small inland resort, with remarkably good shops, pubs and services. It is also one of the few places in the Dales where you could be recommended to come without a car, because public transport services, especially in the summer months, radiate out from the little town in almost every direction, allowing you, if you are prepared to use a bus timetable and a little care, to reach almost any part of the Dales.

Not that you need to travel too far from Grassington. Superb walks start from the town square, and another important factor is the range of possibilities available from full-scale mountain hikes to a modest couple of miles away from the car.

To give you an idea of how this choice operates there are no less than five different routes to the next village, Hebden, all of them delightful, and more or less direct. You could for instance, follow the riverside to Grassington Mill, continuing by the river to the suspension bridge, then follow the charming path up Hebden Gill; or leave the riverside path near Linton Church stepping-stones and make for a field path above Lythe House, the old parishioners' way to Hebden; or go from High Lane, Grassington, by High Cross Farm and the hospital grounds to Hebden; or from High Lane take a lovely high field path by Edge Side and Wise House above the hospital to Garnshaw and Hebden; or climb up to Edge Lane, with its panoramic views, by the new television mast before descending into Hebden Gill at Hole Bottom, and along the lane to Hebden village. This choice gives a number of combinations for an afternoon's walk, possibilities that can be modified to take account of time and inclination.

Grassington stands, in fact, in the off-centre of a semicircle of charming Dales villages – Conistone, Kilnsey, Threshfield, Cracoe, Linton, Thorpe, Burnsall and Hebden, all historic, and very beautiful, most of them with pleasant country pubs that offer an attractive point of call, or local shops that offer some form of refreshment to break a journey. You can, with a local footpath map, take in several of these in a short day's walk, and the combination of field path, riverside and fascinating village is an irresistible one.

Linton, for example, around its large village green, with its three bridges, two for those on foot and one for vehicles, and baroque eighteenth-century almshouses, Fountaines Hospital, is rightly regarded as one of the loveliest of all villages in Craven. There is a direct path from the "Tin Bridge" and falls just below the main Grassington car park, or you can take a slightly longer detour, perhaps including a visit to the ancient parish church of Linton that served the outlying civil parishes, including Grassington, climbing up to Stickhaw Hill (lovely views along the Wharfe) and entering Linton by Crook Lathe and the rear of the camp school. A lovely meandering field path, slightly elevated, crosses by Langerton to Threapland, for Cracoe, from where you can return back along the bottom, an old lake, by the quarry. But for a really interesting and unexpected route take the path from Far Langerton along the side of Elbolton, another reef knoll and site of many prehistoric finds in its caves, before descending, suddenly, into the hamlet of Thorpe, the "hidden village" tucked in a narrow fold of the hills between the reef knolls, a perfect setting for a perfect grey stone village. You can either return to Grassington along the back lane to Waddy Lathe, picking up a little medieval enclosed bridleway down to Stickhaw, or continue eastwards to Burnsall, along an attractive field path, with many stiles to cross, by Skulberts Hill to the centre of Burnsall. The riverside path by Loup Scar will get you back to Grassington.

Threshfield is reached easily enough from Grassington by the bridleway from the old Threshfield Grammar School near Linton Falls, and from there field paths continue to Skythorns and a whole network of paths across Threshfield and Linton Moors towards Bordley. Best of all, perhaps, is a lovely path beyond Wood Nook caravan site along the open and scattered woodland around Rowley Beck that eventually leads up past Bordley Circle and Bordley towards Malham; or you can head northwards over the bleak tops of Kilnsey Moor to join Mastiles Lane into Kilnsey.

Mastiles Lane, is, of course, perhaps the most famous of all the drove-roads in the Pennines, if only owing to the fact of the bitter controversy caused by plans, in the mid-sixties, to tarmacadam its surface for motor traffic. It is a highly satisfying walk between Upper Wharfedale and Malhamdale, starting from behind the Tenant's Arms at Kilnsey Crag (a valuable connecting path from Conistone runs from Conistone Bridge), past the old hall and the fragment of gatehouse of the monastic grange, to climb under Cool Scar and onto Kilnsey Moor. Fragments of monastic cross bases can still be found by the side of the old green way. At Smearbottoms Lane you can either follow the track down to Gordale Lane, or keep straight ahead, up High Bank, to Malham Tarn, and, if you have energy, along across The Streets to Ribblesdale.

North of Grassington, on the Wharfe, is the enchantingly lovely Ghaistrills Strid, a miniature, and less treacherous version of the Bolton Abbey Strid. The riverside path goes through the edge of Grass Wood, a beautiful native woodland, rich in wild flowers. You can return to Grassington along a well-waymarked path through the centre of Grass Wood, a delicious experience. Grass Wood is that rare and precious combination, a limestone woodland. It is a nature reserve of national importance. Please keep to the main paths through the wood and respect its ecological importance. The main path emerges at Park Stile and joins a pleasant path back to Town Head, Grassington.

From Grassington the true mountain limestone begins. Indeed the contrast between the dry-stone walls of dark gritstone and then of pale limestone gives immediate clue to change in underlying strata, and with it a change of the whole character of the country, from the predominantly rather bleak, acid moorland south of Grassington, to the lighter, more fertile high limestone terraces and pastures to the north.

What can one say about limestone country, except that it offers the loveliest walking? Short, closely grazed pastures, white crags, boulders, pavements jutting through this bright green cover to give vivid contrast and dramatic interest, with frequent little caves or shake holes to add to the interest, and, in spring and summer, the unforgettable smell of sweet herbs wherever you go.

Try, for example, the path from the end of Chapel Street, Grassington, by Town Head Farm onto Lea Green, behind Bastow Wood, that crosses Dib Scar into Conistone. You can, in fact, follow the path through the steep crevice of Gurling Trough onto Conistone Dib and come back along a fine high-level path back to Lea Green, but for a real experience of limestone terrace walking at its finest keep straight ahead by the craggy outcrops of Hill Castle Scar, above Swinebar Scar. From here you walk on a high level, with stunning views along the whole dale, across the huge massy bulk of Kilnsey Crag, and along what seems to be the whole length of Littondale. This path descends into Kettlewell by Scar Gill House, with a choice of riverside or a path by the edge of small meadows into Kettlewell village where, if you have checked your bus timetable, there might be a bus back to Grassington.

Totally different is Grassington Moor, easily reached by footpath or car along Moor Lane, at Yarnbury. This is wild, unforgiving country, civilization's end. The area around Yarnbury is packed with ancient workings, and deep and dangerous shafts, some of them partially concealed, remains of the great Wharfedale lead-mining and smelting industry, where, up to the 1880s the entire moorland was filled with activity: water-wheels, wire ropes, canals and buckets of ore. Dwindling veins and cheap imports killed the industry. But a short trail around some of the more impressive remains is being organized, and you can wander up to the gaunt chimney, with its miles of complex flue tunnels, and marvel at the complexity of the engineering and industry which once existed on the now silent moor.

Such a visit could, in fact, combine very well with a visit to Hebden Gill, the steep little valley which runs down from the lead-mining area, becoming ever prettier as it descends into Hebden. Or you can take a number of moorland footpaths heading eastwards towards Grimwith and over some of the high tarns that once supplied the old mills with their great crushers and wheels.

This is, on the high moor, desolate country indeed, the loneliest in England. One track from Conistone, easily reached from Grassington along a connecting path via Bare House (pronounced "Barras") winds up through Mossdale Caverns, scene of a tragic caving accident some years ago, over Conistone Moor and the side of Meugher to descend into Stean, Upper Nidderdale, one of the wildest and loneliest walks in the Pennines. If you plan your day carefully, you might be able on a summer Sunday, to pick up an early evening bus from Middlesmoor or Lofthouse back to Grassington. This is difficult and dangerous country, with walking over rough tussocks and bad and boggy land that makes it tough going. If you are for heroics choose long summer days, tell people where you are going and have a decent compass with you.

Moving north up dale is Kettlewell, another of those lead-mining villages situated on the Wharfe and by a tributary beck that seems to have been arranged in order to fill a photographer's lens. If there is not quite the variety of walks from Kettlewell as from Grassington, it is, nevertheless, a splendid centre.

Perhaps the best walk of all from Kettlewell is the one which follows the steep and well-waymarked path over Gate Close Scar into Littondale. It is a splendid climb, a near scramble up a little nick and then up a seemingly never-ending series of massive steps onto Old Cote Moor. But the views are truly magnificent and, offer that marvellous and typical Dales thrill of crossing the bleak fell summit and looking down into the next dale, an experience which never dulls. The path descends into Arncliffe through a beautiful hanging wood, one of the several relict woodlands in Littondale that are survivors of ancient forests. From Arncliffe a riverside path returns to Hawkswick and another beautiful path along and over the nose of Knipe Scar with, as you would expect, views right down dale to Kilnsey Crag and Grass Wood, before descending over limestone pasture and scattered woodland back to Kettlewell.

There are, of course, attractive riverside walks from Kettlewell, the Dales Way to Starbotton and Buckden. You can return from Starbotton by woodland and field path on the far side of the river or best of all along the bridleway that climbs Arncliffe, the old postman's path, leaving it to contour the ridge past Moor End Farm and descend into Kettlewell which forms an elevation that offers quite perfect views of the village. Or, if you have but an hour to spare, walk downstream from Kettlewell Bridge, on either bank, to the new stepping-stones, and back along the other side.

Other attractive possibilities include following the old lead-miners' path from the eastern edge of the village – follow Cam Gill Beck – to Providence Pot, perhaps climbing up the old lead workings to join the old turf road to the south back to the village, or up the fine old Top Mere Road to the top of Cam Head – again glorious views, then back into Kettlewell along the green way known as the Starbotton Road zigzagging down into Starbotton.

The classic mountain walk from Kettlewell is, of course, to Great Whernside, and the best ascent of this is undoubtedly to follow Top Mere Road to Cam Head, bearing right to the prehistoric Tor Dyke on the Park Rash Road. A bridleway climbs the shoulder of the fell, ahead, but open access is tolerated here, and many walkers make their way up to the long, craggy summit of Great Whernside, really a long and rocky ridge, giving views to the east across the Nidderdale Moors, crossed by the bridleway on its way to Little Whernside and Angram Reservoir, and looking west back across Wharfedale to Old Cote Moor.

Great Whernside is a very satisfactory mountain, gaunt and lean, but giving the walker a true sense of purpose, and at 704 metres (2,304 feet) the highest summit in Wharfedale. The best descent into Kettlewell is by Hag Dyke and the footpath back to the village, but interesting alternatives exist.

And finally, Buckden. To a degree Buckden relates as much to Langstrothdale and Littondale as the rest of Wharfedale, though the riverside path (the Dales Way) from Kettlewell and Starbotton is a splendid route, and again, by using the bus timetable you can

Barden Bridge, Wharfedale

Grassington, Wharfedale

Gritstone country – Rylstone Cross

Limestone country – above Conistone, Upper Wharfedale

Arncliffe, Littondale

In Ellerdale – woodland path near Cracoe

Leeds–Liverpool Canal — Gargrave locks

Malham Cove

Malham Tarn from Nappa Cross

Hull Pot, Ribblesdale

*Thorns Gill,
Ribblesdale*

In Crummackdale

Whernside

Ingleborough from Kingsdale

combine such a walk with time for a pint or a coffee in the village before the bus down dale. There is an excellent car park in the village and Buckden Pike is an obvious target for many walkers starting from there. Unfortunately there is no right of way up the most obvious track from Buckden to the pike, up the gill past the lead mines to the summit. The route therefore is along the Roman road from the car park, bearing right up the fields to the summit ridge, and along the top to the trig. station.

Like Great Whernside, Buckden Pike offers splendid views in all directions, and has the feel of a genuine mountain; it is a curious feature of Dales geomorphology that the summits of the Dales are mostly within a hundred feet or so of each other in height, so that as you stand on a rounded top, the other whale-back summits come into view, indeed like a great school of stone whales frozen in space and time.

Descend Buckden Pike by the Walden Road, a green way which leaves the summit ridge to its immediate south, an easy and pleasant walk down to Starbottom, then along the riverside back to Buckden. But if you have time and energy, and are prepared to stay overnight or work out transport, (weekend service 800 goes along the main road below West Burton) you can undertake one of the most marvellous walks in the Dales, a route for the real connoisseur, to descend wild and rough country into the secet valley of Walden.

And indeed, on the subject of inter-dale routes, there are few more satisfying ways than that from Buckden along the Roman road to Cray to pick up the continuation of that road over the Stake Pass and the watershed to the ruined church of Stalling Busk and Semerwater. Again, time the walk carefully, and the 800 bus will return you to a parked car from Bainbridge.

Littondale and Langstrothdale
Littondale, Kingsley's Vendale from *The Water Babies*, has everything a paradise should – steep valley sides with hanging woods, rich pasture in the valley floor, wild flowers and two delightful villages with equally delightful pubs.

But it is not a valley for short circular walks. There are no large car parks (and you will not be thanked for cluttering up the village green at Arncliffe), no shops and no public loos; its real magic emerges for the rambler on longer, wilder walks, crossing out of

Wharfedale, Langstrothdale or Malhamdale. A number of quite spectacular passes lead out of Littondale, but all require a full day's walk and careful planning if you want to avoid merely retracing your steps. There is the old green way from Arncliffe Cote along Cote Gill which, though it is not obvious on OS maps, is in fact a public road and a glorious ramble to Malham Tarn. Even finer, is the old Monk's Way, up behind the Falcon Inn in Arncliffe which climbs dizzily up behind Yew Cogar Scar with Alpine steepness, following a natural pass over the limestone through Clowder and Middle House, an ancient settlement above Malham Tarn. There is the direct old postman's and parson's path from Arncliffe by Brayshaw Scar climbing over the top of Old Cote Moor to Starbotton, or, perhaps loveliest of all, take the valley bottom path up to Litton and pick up the bridle-path by the Queen's Arms that climbs steeply up, with ever more splendid views of all the Dales peaks, over Capple Stones, and a long, exhilarating slope to Redmire and the woods west of Buckden.

Going further north to Halton Gill, a famous pack-horse way zigzags up to Horse Head Pass and over the summit to Raisgill, in Langstrothdale, whilst due north, a little-used footpath crosses the same moor to Beckermonds.

It is therefore possible to plan a very enjoyable, though fairly strenuous day, starting either from Buckden or Litton and by crossing the fells twice, enjoy a circular walk which takes in both Dales, connecting the chosen passes by lengths of lovely riverside paths. Be it said that it takes a little moorland physical toughness having climbed one fellside, a good thousand feet from green valley floor to moorland top, to start back on the second climb up. Access along the ridge top, tempting as it is a second long haul, is limited and farmers are rightly sensitive about walkers climbing their walls and leaving gates open.

An alternative way out of Littondale is into Ribblesdale. From Foxup a track and ancient road flanks the north side of Pen y Ghent to emerge at Hull Pot and Horton, whilst from Litton, the grassy track from New Bridge follows the south side of Pen y Ghent Gill to join the road to Stainforth near Dalehead. From here paths cross the shoulder of Pen y Ghent to Helwith Bridge and Horton.

Undoubtedly the best way to enjoy these splendid moorland

passes is to leave a car at Skipton, or travel all the way by public transport, and catch an early bus to Kilnsey, Kettlewell or Buckden (on occasions Arncliffe) and after crossing into Littondale, head for Malhamdale or Ribblesdale for buses and (from Ribblesdale) trains back to Skipton and West Yorkshire. This is all classic fell walking country and deserves the time and energy to plan such a day out away from the tyranny of the car.

Langstrothdale, however, offers some gentler routes. An extremely inviting walk can be enjoyed by following the Roman road from Buckden car park to Cray, and, if you can resist too long a stay at the White Lion, continue either down Cray Gill to Hubberholme, a lovely path with waterfalls, or along the top of Hubberholme Wood before descending to Yockenthwaite, then back along a lovely piece of riverside to Hubberholme with its ancient church, containing one of the very few rood-loft screens in England, its George Inn, and, a quarter of a mile down the lane, a riverside path that emerges at Buckden Bridge.

The higher stretches of Langstrothdale by the Bronze Age circle, another waymark on an ancient trans-Pennine trade route, to Deepdale and on to Beckermonds are of course, very fine. But you must either retrace your steps, or, in a more energetic mood continue to Oughtershaw and Cam along the Dales Way and climb over to Littondale or perhaps follow the land through Greenfield which soon becomes a track leading into Ribblesdale.

You are now in the heartland of the Yorkshire Dales, a wild, remote area of barren moorlands, infant streams and a sense all around you of space, light and long and empty horizons. Who said Britain is an overcrowded country? It is not up near the source of the Wharfe and the watershed of all England where, within a few miles, all the Dales and all the rivers, in the emptiness and the silence, seem to begin.

REFERENCE

Maps

Ordnance Survey Landranger 1:50,000 Sheet 98 Wensleydale and Wharfedale; 99 Northallerton and Ripon; 104 Leeds and Bradford

Ordnance Survey Outdoor Leisure 1:25,000 Malham and Upper Wharfedale

The Bolton Abbey Footpath Map, Arthur Gemmell (Stile Maps)
The Ilkley Moor Footpath Map and Guide (Ramblers Association)
The Grassington Footpath Map, Arthur Gemmell (Stile Maps)

Books
Upper Wharfedale, F. W. Houghton (Dalesman, 1980)
Parklink Walks in Upper Wharfedale (includes maps), Arthur Gemmell (Stile Maps, 1978)
Walking in the Craven Dales, Colin Speakman (Dalesman, 1973)
Walking in Lower Wharfedale, Geoffrey White (Dalesman, 1980)
Walking in Upper Wharfedale, Mike Obst (Dalesman, 1980)
Walks for Motorists in the Yorkshire Dales, Ramblers Association West Riding Area (Warne, 1980)

5

Ellerdale and Malhamdale

In his *Chronicles and Stories of the Craven Dales*, James Henry Dixon, the nineteenth-century scholar and wit, used the delightful name Ellerdale for the country immediately north of Skipton, around the Ellerbeck and on the Flasby Fells; a good name, so why not revive it?

Further west, the Aire has two more tributaries, Eshton Beck and Winterburn Beck which again run through countryside of great character, before the main river twists northwards at Coniston Cold into Malhamdale.

The stunning beauty of Malham and its environs needs no more emphasis here; with Bolton Abbey it is perhaps the most heavily visited village of the Yorkshire Dales and offers glories that cannot be denied. But the danger of a showpiece area, which Malham undoubtedly is, lies in the fact that the area immediately adjacent to it is often unjustly overlooked. Which is, in a way, as well, because not so far from the major tourist trails are some delectable footpaths, landscape of soft charm and subtle character, green, gentle, rolling drumlins and scattered woodlands which, if they existed in almost any other area, would be overrun by visitors.

So a section of the Dales of great contrast: rather gentle, charming countryside bounded by such villages as Hetton, Rylstone, Flasby, Winterburn, Carlton, Gargrave, Airton, Coniston Cold, Otterburn and Hellifield, where you will not often see too many other walkers; and then Malham itself, all drama and spectacle, where all the world seems to converge.

But this is by no means a question of hard choices. Choose your day with care, and if it is a sunny Sunday afternoon, or Bank Holiday week, discover the quieter paths. Enjoy the spectacular crags and scars, which are, let it be said, among the best in the

British Isles, when you will not have to queue to get over a stile. Even in Gordale or Malham Cove that is most of the year.

Ellerdale

There are some very rewarding walks from Skipton, which, because it is so well served by public transport (frequent rail service and bus services from West Yorkshire into the sur-rounding Dales), makes an admirable starting-point for any walk, with always the possibility of a bus back from the outward point to a parked car, or through-transport home. Indeed, given its nodal position in Dales transport services, with trains along both the Settle–Carlisle and the Morecambe line via Giggleswick, and buses to Upper Wharfedale, Malhamdale, Ribblesdale, Ingleton and even, in the season, to Wensleydale and Swaledale, Skipton could be an excellent choice for anyone wanting to stay in the Dales for a week or more and explore the region on foot and by public transport. The town has, moreover, excellent shops, pubs, a magnificent medieval castle, a canal with a towpath, ample car parks and a lot of character (strongly Dales but with more than a hint of Lancashire).

But to consider walks from Skipton itself. If you have only an hour to spare, follow the High Street beyond the church to the canal bridge just before the Gargrave road junction, and take the path, right, from the bridge along the towpath of the disused Springs Branch of the Leeds–Liverpool Canal, that runs behind Skipton Castle, originally built to serve an old stone quarry. Ellerbeck runs on the other side of the path through an attractive glade. Where the path crosses the beck to join a track, above, turn right to enter Skipton Woods, or more correctly Castle Woods (open afternoons only 2p.m.–6p.m.or dusk). The path through the woods follows the beck up and around the Round Dam, and forms a delightful stroll.

The Leeds–Liverpool Canal is, of course, a major piece of industrial archaeology as well as being an important waterway for leisure craft. It is, in fact, the oldest and the only surviving trans-Pennine waterway, dating from the 1770s and with much of the original lock and canal side machinery in operation. It is basically a contour canal, relying on the natural lie of the land and Aire Gap through the Pennines rather than the expensive locks and elaborate machinery of later canal engineers which proved

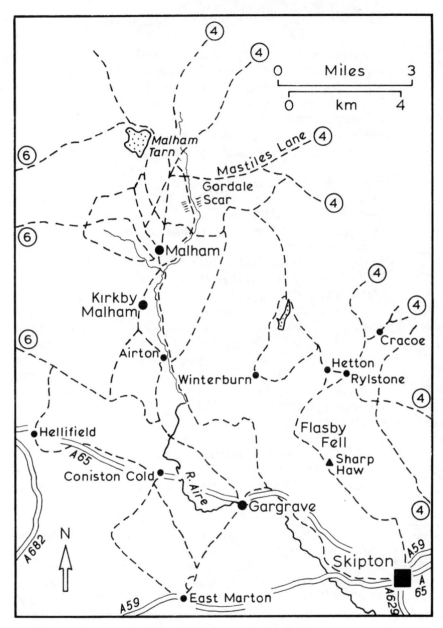

ELLERDALE AND MALHAMDALE

more expensive to maintain and to supply with water. The towpath makes a most intriguing walk for anyone interested in canals, industrial history, boats or wildlife or who is merely looking for an almost perfectly level path (the exception is the occasional gentle slope by a lock).

The whole canal and wharf complex in Skipton is worthy of exploration, but if you want to get onto the main towpath, join it at the far side of Belmont Bridge on the Colne Road, and follow it westwards by factories, terraces and allotments winding its way in true contour canal fashion along the very edge of the higher land, often close to the River Aire and offering fine views of the surrounding hills. Gargrave with its first locks, was once a busy canal port and had important wharves where lead from Grassington Moor mines was loaded for export via Liverpool.

Buses and trains will get you back to Skipton, or you can take a pleasant field path behind the church, which runs parallel with the railway line direct to Skipton. In fact, however, the loveliest section of the entire Leeds–Liverpool Canal's one hundred and twenty-seven miles lies ahead of you, winding past the locks and boatyards of Bank Newton, around a most extraordinarily long loop to Langber and East Marton with its strange double-arch bridge on the A59. This section can be combined with a return trip along the Pennine Way going northwards from East Marton back to Gargrave.

But to return to Ellerdale. A classic walk is from Skipton over Sharp Haw. From the junction with the Gargrave and Grassington roads follow the lane uphill past Leat's Mill (a little water-mill museum worth a visit if time permits) up Chapel Hill to a stile by an antique cast-iron footpath sign. The path goes straight ahead across Park Hill and Old Park, now dissected by the new Skipton bypass. Cross the road with care and continue over the golf course to Brackenley Lane. From here the route is westwards to the Grassington Road, by field paths north of Tarn House, then, winding up the Stirton Lane, take a track by a field gate, leaving it as the track bears left to follow the path up the open fell, a long, rather dull plod up Skyrakes to the summit of Sharp Haw ahead.

Sharp Haw, like Beamsley Beacon, is another of those modest Dales summits whose rewards are out of all proportion to the effort required. It offers a superb viewpoint across the Aire Gap, into the hills of the South Pennines and the Bowland Fells, and northwards into Malhamdale where, if the sun is shining, the white clints of the high pavements and the face of the Cove gleam like distant ice.

Take care when descending to keep to the east of High Wood, on the Rough Haw side, to join an old, enclosed lane into the hamlet of Flasby.

The most direct way to Rylstone from here is along the track past Flasby Moorside; but the most pleasant route is undoubtedly along Hetton Beck, turning right through a gate at the farm at Flasby, and tracing the path through a narrow and hidden valley, to a point south of Hetton where you can either fork left, uphill, to Hetton and its Angel Inn, or cross a foot-bridge over the beck, climbing uphill to the Swinden branch railway and track into Rylstone.

Buses return from Hetton and Rylstone to Skipton, but Rylstone, with its ornamental pond, offers many intriguing possibilities. Take time to explore its little church, before perhaps continuing (through a wicket-gate beyond the farm) to Cracoe along an ancient green lane, or, if you are returning towards Skipton, a field path just north of the church leads to the old pre-turnpike road for the old toll-house at Sandy Beck Bar.

Or, you can climb up onto Rylstone Fell, part of the Barden Moor Access Area, perhaps taking the old bridleway past Norton Tower, that tragic reminder of the ill-fated Norton family who perished in the rising of the North in 1569, perhaps making for Rylstone Cross, a splendid viewpoint, or following the moor edge, past Waterfall Gill to Crookrise Crag, another dramatic viewpoint, before descending past Embsay reservoir for Embsay and Skipton.

This is all landscape of great romantic beauty, jagged crags, wooded escarpments, rocky knolls, an area charged with historic association and atmosphere.

The existence of a reasonably good bus service on the Skipton–Grassington road allows the rambler to plan a variety of longer or shorter walks without having to depend on circular trips back to a parked car.

From Cracoe, for example, a bridleway along a green lane begins near the crossroads with the Gargrave road and climbs up, past Ratts Lathe onto Linton Moor. A track along Eller Beck (not the original Eller Beck, but a tributary of the Wharfe – ellers simply means alders) leads directly to Linton. Or, bearing south-west beyond Hammerton Hill, you will find a track crosses Boss Moor heading for Winterburn Reservoir, from where you can return directly to Hetton along Moor Lane.

The little valley formed by Winterburn Beck is another delight-ful small area to explore. An excellent walk can be enjoyed by parking on the broad lane leading up to Winterburn Reservoir, near the old chapel, and following the wooded track almost to the reservoir dam, then the farm track to Way Gill, continuing past High Cow House to the head of the reservoir, originally a feeder for the Leeds–Liverpool canal and now an important sanctuary for bird life. A moorland track, marked by gates, crosses the low hill to Owslin Laithe and the road back to Winterburn.

Malhamdale

For convenience, let us assume that Malhamdale begins at Gar-grave. Gargrave is a useful centre for walking, with a very good bus and rail service from West Yorkshire, ample cafés, pubs, shops, and car parking. It is, of course, on the Pennine Way, and few pleasanter walks can be imagined than simply following the way from Gargrave to Malham (see Chapter 13).

A different and equally charming way of discovering this section of Malhamdale is to take the old lane followed by the Pennine Way from Gargrave past Gargrave House, but to keep on it over Heber Hill up to Crag Laithe (laithe, by the by, is Old Norse for a barn), and on to Bell Busk.

Bell Busk used to be the railway station for Malham, remaining open right until the 1950s. The station is now a private house, but almost opposite the old station drive, a bridleway goes by the farmyard at Raven Flatt due north, crossing a bridge and bearing left up to Well Head Lathe and Kirk Syke, to Airton.

Return to Gargrave by the Pennine Way, but, on the low ridge beyond Newfield Hall, bear north past Throstle Nest Farm, following the lane past St Helen's Well (an ancient pagan well now lost under efficient and hygienic water board extracting equipment) across Nappa Bridge to an idyllic path that climbs past the Jacobean farm at Brockabank, over Winterburn Beck. Keep straight ahead to find a path that leaves the farm track and, in the same direction (looking for kissing gate in the corner of the wood) goes directly through Eshton Park to Gargrave.

Airton, higher up Malhamdale, has some good routes to the head of the dale; the village has not much room for car parking, (or other facilities) but for public transport users or if you have walked from Gargrave, you can thread your way northwards either through the network of field paths above Scosthrop and Kirkby Malham, or for something really dramatic, follow the lane up to Calton village and take the marvellous bridleway along the broad Calton Moor ridge. This track is not easy to discern on the ground – take a mid-point between High Field Syke and the wall to your left, climbing up hill, again with the wall and parish boundary as your bearing, to the open fell, a hard slog up to Weets Cross, a focal point for the moorland boundaries of many parishes, and the stump of a monastic cross high above. Paths radiate from this historic point: back along Whetstone Gill to Winterburn and Hetton, due east to Bordley for Threshfield and Wharfedale, north to Mastiles Lane and Malham Tarn. But most people will be content to trundle down Gordale Lane to Malham.

A careful check with a local bus timetable will indicate useful late afternoon buses on Sundays as well as weekdays back to Gargrave and Skipton.

Malham, inevitably, is the focal point for a number of famous and dramatic walks around the head of the dale. And understandably; the existence of the Craven Faults to the north of the village has created a small area which, in microcosm, illustrates all the typical and most splendid features of karst scenery in the United Kingdom, and one needs little understanding of geology to respond to the sheer theatre of crag thrust above crag, and the resonance of lovely pale rock, so responsive to sunlight that on bright clear days, natural colours seems to have an even greater intensity.

The village has a purpose-built information centre and large car park to entrap the motorist as he arrives. To put it plain, it caters for tourists. Pubs, cafés and shops cater for the tidal wave of visitors that arrive each season, some of them knowing what to do when they arrive, others simply drifting through because they have heard the name and think it worth a visit.

You can, with only a couple of hours to spare, enjoy three of Malham's great show-pieces in a walk of about three miles from the car park. Take the main Cove Road up past Town Head Farm, then along the newly constructed path direct to the Cove; alternatively, a quieter path, over stiles, goes along the other side of Malham Beck starting at the lane past the youth hostel, and leading to the foot-bridge below the Cove.

The Cove, some 240 feet high, of pure "Great Scar" limestone is generally believed to be the result of a primeval waterfall eroding the fault scar, carving out the characteristic lip. The dark stains on the rock are a form of lichen. It is, by common consent, an impressive sight. The route up the side of the Cove is marked by steps constructed by the National Park service to reduce the erosion, and stabilize the soft clays. Follow the path, the Pennine Way, onto the intriguing limestone pavement, that characteristic plateau of clints and grykes (grykes are the hollows between the clints) along the top of the Cove, with its justifiably famous view down Malhamdale and across the Aire Gap to Pendle. Follow the path across the stile in the far wall, climbing uphill and bearing right to Shortley Hill and the lane. Cross over – almost directly ahead, another stile leads to the path behind Cawden Hill, well waymarked through to Gordale Bridge. Ahead is the path to Gordale Scar.

How can one do justice to Gordale Scar in a handful of words? Gordale is one of the most famous natural wonders of all England, a site of pilgrimage for the great and famous – see James Ward's magnificent painting in the Tate Gallery – a cult amongst painters, travellers and aesthetes at the turn of the nineteenth century, when they would come to stand under the cataract, shudder with horror and, in a spirit of Gothic delight, scramble up the falls enjoying every moment of terror.

It once was considered a collapsed cavern; the current theory is that it is the result of retreating glacial melt-waters carving through a weakness in the rock, which centuries of erosion by the beck has increased. No matter the theory; in practice it is an awesome place, a dark, brooding ravine, whose little yews growing in high niches and rocky shelves do nothing to lighten. The waterfall, a fast cascade, tumbles under a natural arch of rock, over an apron of limestone deposit or tufa, splashing and whirling down the central sections, leaving another mass of tufa deposit. It is a strange, atmospheric place, echoey, weird, best visited early or late in the year when most visitors are safely at home, perhaps when the sky is grey and dull, and the beck is in spate, and no one else is about. It has that rare quality, something the Romantic poets have taught us to appreciate, of the sublime, a sense of the tragic grandeur and power of nature, something greater and more sombre than mere mankind.

Mankind is, however, nibbling away at Gordale with hundreds of tiny feet, scrambling up the vulnerable tufa, wearing the rocks smooth, creating a slippery scree slope in the dry valley above. It is a bit like scrambling up the side of Westminster Abbey. There is, of course, a public right of way up Gordale waterfall. You can exercise your rights, and an exciting scramble it is. But perhaps the interests of a unique and precious asset are better served by standing at the foot, soaking in the atmosphere, occasionally the spray of the waterfall, and marvelling.

The return to Malham is best achieved by the footpath past Janet's Foss. Janet's Foss is reached by the path that starts at the gateway just beyond Gordale Bridge – the Foss is a charming little waterfall, originally called Gennet's Foss (of which "Janet" is an uncouth modern corruption). According to the more fanciful nineteenth-century topographers, Gennet was a local fairy who dwelt in the little cave behind the waterfall. With its single skirt of water overlooking a small, still, pool, it is a beautiful place, as is the woodland through which your path descends, following Gordale Beck right through along a shallow valley to join the Pennine Way south of Malham. This path is the result of a recent diversion and is not shown on all Ordnance maps. Follow the signs and waymarks back into Malham.

The other great magnet of the Malham area is, of course, Malham Tarn; that lovely, at least semi-natural stretch of water. Such a lake might astonish in the heart of limestone country, where natural sink holes and soakaways usually ensure that most streams, let alone lakes, rapidly vanish underground. But Malham Tarn lies on a floor of impervious Silurian slates, exposed here by the North Craven Fault, with the clays of a glacial moraine impounding the water to create one of the jewels of the Pennines.

A fine walk from Malham Cove to the tarn is to follow the dry valley (Watlowes) from immediately above the Cove, which runs up past Comb Scar to the tarn. A bridleway goes round the tarn and through the woods around Tarn House. These woods – like the whole surrounding area National Trust land – are an important nature reserve and wildlife sanctuary, but a nature trail leaflet is usually on sale to explain some of the features of the natural history. Call in at Tarn House for details of the many specialist and introductory courses in natural history that are available from the Field Studies Centre there.

Return to Malham past the Water Sinks (where the stream from the tarn, Malham Water, reappears below Malham at Aire Head Springs, not beneath the Cove as you might expect) to join the Pennine Way along Trougate, another dry valley, or choose one of the paths across Prior Rakes, the name of the pasture giving vivid clue to the monastic ownership of the area in medieval times.

The temptation to descend to Malham via Gordale is to be avoided. By all means go that way to the tarn if you choose, but the descent is in certain conditions, downright dangerous, especially when the rocks are wet, and is very much more difficult than the ascent. Descending ramblers, moreover, cause more damage and erosion than when ascending.

This entire area in the triangle between Cove, scar and tarn is, in effect, one major archaeological site, with Bronze Age hut circles and masses of ancient Iron Age Celtic fields, visible in the afternoon like a patchwork quilt; of medieval reins and lynchets, monastic shepherd huts and enclosures. But, as the gaunt smelt-mill chimney on Malham Moor testifies, there are remains of more recent activities of man in the Malham area. For some insight into this, take the path to the east of Malham village, reached from the old unsurfaced lane behind the car park by Burns Barn and the splendid Great Heads Barn. Look for a stile immediately past the point where the track fords a beck. The path climbs the side of Pikedaw Hill, virtually along the Mid-Craven Fault line, the contrast between dark gritstone and pale limestones being particularly marked. The path passes remains of lead-mine workings, including a fine adit or horizontal drain dated 1872. There are excellent views from here along the fault line to Cawden and Gordale. The path crosses the wall enclosing Pikedaw and climbs up to join the old Settle–Malham drove-road, the road used by Dorothy and William Wordsworth on their visit to Malham and Gordale in 1807. Just west of the signpost where the Pikedaw path meets the ancient green track is the entrance to the calamine shaft, leading to a deep cavern where, in the last century, calamine, a zinc ore, was mined and used for brass manufacture and paint making.

You can either return directly to Malham village from this point, (a beautiful zigzagging path to the Cove Road) or, continuing westwards, pick up the path for Langscar Gate past Nappa Cross, another of those wayside crosses erected by the careful Cistercians to ensure the assistance of the Almighty and also create a useful, clearly visible waymark. From Nappa Cross, or indeed anywhere from the Settle–Malham drove-road, there are quite breathtaking views over the great scars and pavements above Malham, and, most satisfying of all, the still mirror glass of Malham Tarn, catching the light and the reflection of its backcloth of trees. The Langscar Gate path joins an old green lane (a country road) back to the Cove Road, from where you can join the path down Watlowes or the dry valley back to the Cove.

Many splendid walks can be planned, of course, by following the tracks from Malhamdale to Upper Wharfedale and Littondale as suggested in the last chapter, but also, continuing further westwards, to Ribblesdale. The Malham–Settle track described above does offer a magnificent cross-dale route, emerging on the lane by Stockdale Farm, from where a little natural pass can be followed between Sugar Loaf Hill and Attermine to permit a quite thrilling descent over what feels to be the roof-tops of Settle, coming so suddenly as you do into Ribblesdale with the town nestling below you.

But the Langscar Gate track offers a splendid way over Gorbeck and Langcliffe Scar to Langcliffe, with connecting paths from the tarn crossroads and from Capon Hall.

Energetic walkers can, in fact, plan great days crossing right over from Wharfedale to Ribblesdale, a good score of miles but with everything to offer in terms of fine country and strong contrasts of scenery. For those seeking such delights, from a wide choice, I would select two outstanding routes, Kettlewell to Arncliffe up the Nick and over Old Cote Moor; Arncliffe to Middle House by Yew Cogar Scar to Malham; then Capon Hall to Langcliffe – great walking throughout. This is not difficult to plan. Leave early, park your car at Skipton to catch an early weekday bus to Kettlewell. You will be in Settle with excellent time for a meal before catching the evening train back to Skipton.

My second choice would start in Ribblesdale, this time from the morning train to Settle, over the drove-road to Malham, by Janet's Foss and Gordale to Weets Top, over the moor to Bordley and by Height Lathe and Rowley Beck to Skythorns and Thresh-field; again glorious and varied tramping, with time for a meal and a pint before a late bus down the valley.

These are vintage rambles for long days to be planned, executed and treasured in memory for years afterwards; but the western fringes of Malhamdale have some pleasing country which offers interesting afternoons and even shorter winter days to relish. You can, for example, with the assistance of the Malhamdale Footpath Map, plan an interesting afternoon taking the path from Malham down the western side of the beck by the old mill to Hanlith Bridge and Kirkby Malham, then following the lane up Micklaw to pick up the path by Acraplatts, and a pleasant descent with some unusual views into Malham and across to the Cove.

Or from Kirkby Malham with its fascinating church (Iron Age stone heads built into its walls) take the old church path, Kirk Gait, over Kirk Gait hill to Scosthrop Lane, continuing due south to Park House and down Otterburn Beck to the isolated hamlet of Otterburn. To make a circuit back either follow the lane to Bell Busk or the little used and virtually forgotten path up and between the twin grassy knolls of Kendal Hill past the deserted Kendal House to Bell Busk, picking up the Kirk Syke path from Bell Busk to Airton and Kirkby Malham.

Otterburn lies on an ancient pre-turnpike highway, in existence before the Leeds–Kendal turnpike was built in the eighteenth century. You can still follow this, a deep sunken lane climbing Wenningber Hill and crossing Hellifield Moor Top, with several connecting paths to Hellifield and Long Preston or north to Airton, before it becomes Langbar Lane and descends past the lovely little Scalebar Force to Settle.

This countryside is amongst the least walked and least visited in the Yorkshire Dales, yet is neither difficult of access nor of terrain, offering excellent views across Ribblesdale into Bowland and into the higher reaches of Malhamdale. The existence of regular bus services along the main A65 road and trains to Hellifield make cross-country walks easy to plan, and the low, rounded hillocks formed from glacial drumlins give a quite different feel and flavour to the area.

There is indeed, a lovely triangle of countryside, between Ribble and Aire, contained by the A65, A59 and A682 roads, with

Gargrave, Gisburn, the Martons and Hellifield as its main nodal points. It fringes the Dales, nor quite belongs to Bowland, and yet not quite the South Pennines. Country for the *cognoscenti*, that does not really require publicizing here. So be it; not many ramblers are about in such quiet corners, paths are hard to find. Take your First Series 1:25,000 maps, a compass, and see how you cope.

But here are two easier tasters: go from Hellifield past Hellifield Peel (surely one of the most southerly of all the Border peel towers?) and to High Ground, and back to the A65 road to pick up one of the few paths in Coniston Cold Parish which takes you right past the edge of Coniston Park with a lovely view of the lake.

The second is from Coniston Cold itself. Take the lane by Pot Haw and Moorber Lane by Stainton Cotes to Stainton, and then south-east by Ingthorpe Grange, a seventeenth-century farm-house, to East Marton. There is a choice of Pennine Way or Leeds–Liverpool canal towpath back to Gargrave or forward to Thornton in Craven where regular bus services will soon bring you back to Skipton.

REFERENCE

Maps
Ordnance Survey Landranger 1:50,000 sheet 103 Blackburn and Burnley Ordnance Survey Outdoor Leisure 1:25,000 Malham and Upper Wharfedale
The Malhamdale Footpath Map, Arthur Gemmell (Stile Maps)

Books
Malham and Malham Moor, Arthur Raistrick (Dalesman, 1971)
Parklink Walks in Upper Wharfedale, Arthur Gemmell (Stile, 1978)
Walking in the Craven Dales, Colin Speakman (Dalesman, 1973)
Walking in Malhamdale, Colin Speakman (Dalesman, 1985)

6

Ribblesdale and the Three Peaks

For some unaccountable reason, Ribblesdale tends to get a poor Press among admirers of the Dales. This is, no doubt, owing to the effect of the major quarries which, whilst they add a certain gaunt grandeur to the landscape, a sort of lunar crater effect, do not correspond to most people's ideal of natural beauty.

But there is far more to Ribblesdale than that – a raw, bleak, workaday valley perhaps, but containing much true mountain landscape and, often in quite unexpected places, moments of great charm and softness, not least in the river itself which is swift, vigorous, and often surprisingly pretty, a true mountain river.

Where all concur, however, is in praise of the Three Peaks, Pen y Ghent, Ingleborough, and Whernside, among the most celebrated mountains in England. For mountains unmistakably they are, huge upreared peaks with a sense of drama that belies their relatively modest height above sea-level. It is not surprising that most eighteenth-century topographers regarded Ingleborough as the highest mountain in England.

For simplicity, I shall divide this complex area of the Dales into four sections: firstly the area immediately around and to the north of Settle dominated by the craggy limestone scars of the various Craven Faults. I shall call these the Ribblesdale Edges. Secondly Pen y Ghent and Horton in Ribblesdale. Thirdly, Ingleborough itself, to include Crummackdale, Clapham and Austwick; and finally Whernside including the Chapel le Dale area and the vicinity of Ingleton. There must also remain the question of the Three Peaks Walk.

The Ribblesdale Edges
There is something immensely attractive about Settle, Upper Ribblesdale's principal market town, something reassuring and

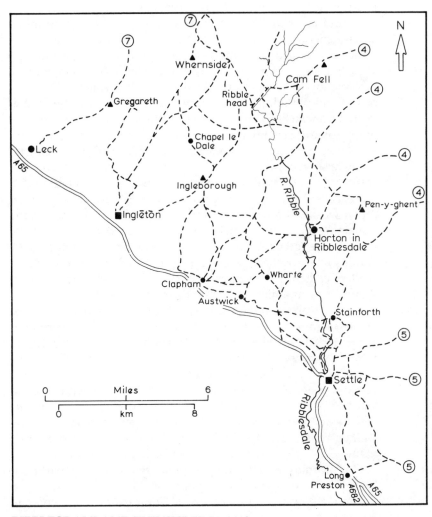

RIBBLESDALE AND THE THREE PEAKS

very English. It has enough about it that is plain and ordinary or even downright dull to save it from becoming preserved in preservationists' aspic, yet has corners of great beauty and character and individuality. The market square is both picturesque and functional – every Tuesday the base of the market pillar is lost under a busy throng of market stalls, produce, and feet and its attractive shops and cafés bring in more than the casual tourists heading for the Lake District or Morecambe Bay. It has a number of very fine buildings, none more impressive than the magnificent Jacobean Folly Hall, on Victoria Street just to the south-east of the square. Several quiet courts and ginnels, with eighteenth- and nineteenth-century buildings and cottages of great character repay observation.

If you have only an hour to spend in Settle, spend part of it in the excellent Museum of North Craven Life in Victoria Street (open weekend afternoons, and daily in the summer) and the remaining time up Castlebergh Hill, reached just behind the town centre (go up Castle Hill behind The Trustee Savings Bank and turn right at the first junction uphill to where a white gate on the left leads to the zigzagging path to the summit) from where there is a panoramic view across the roof-tops of the town.

It is as a starting and finishing point for walks that Settle will be of most significance to readers of this book. And, ramblers' needs are remarkably well catered for. It has, would you believe it, an Inter-City rail service, albeit only two trains in each direction a day, and none on Sundays except on Dales Rail days (see Chapter 14). But a genuine main-line service for all that with through locomotive-hauled trains from Leeds, Appleby and Carlisle, and a station with station staff and a proper booking-office and waiting-room, beautifully kept and indeed restored as part of the 1976–7 centenary celebrations of the Settle–Carlisle line.

The morning and evening express services are a particular boon for walkers planning long days on the tops.

There are also good bus services from Skipton, Ingleton and Lancaster.

Cafés, pubs, a fish and chip shop, and even shops selling rucksacks, boots, spare socks and anoraks, if you have inadvertently left yours at home (and this has happened before now), make the fell walker feel that Settle is a town that is used to ramblers and their ways.

There are, indeed, excellent possibilities for even quite short walks from Settle. Ribblesdale contains some fine country south of Settle and the river skirts the Dales by Gisburn, Hellifield and Long Preston. But this fringes Lancashire, part of the Forest of Bowland, an area different in character and history to the Yorkshire Dales, and, regrettably, beyond the scope of this book.

Our real concern must lie to the north of Settle.

One short but spectacular walk to give a real flavour of the Ribblesdale Edges requires little more than a couple of hours. Go up Constitution Hill, from the north-eastern corner of the market square, forking right up a stony track that quickly becomes a bridleway by a wall, soon forking right again up to the woods above Langcliffe and a track up to Langcliffe Scar. This is a small public access area, and a path, over stiles, goes below the scar – look for a track that climbs up to your left to Victoria Cave, a splendid little viewpoint where early in the last century, major archaeological finds were recorded. The cave was first discovered on the Jubilee Day of Queen Victoria, hence its name. Take care not to cause damage or disturbance to this historic and ecologically sensitive area.

Return to the path below, which goes down a dry valley and into a dramatic little gorge below the towering white crags of Attermire Scar and Warrendale Knotts, limestone outcroppings along the line of the Mid-Craven Fault which give the impression, in miniature, of the Italian Dolomites. The path, which forms part of the ancient drove-road from Settle, turns west between Sugar Loaf Hill and Warrendale Knotts to form a gated green way zigzagging down steeply into the Langcliffe track from Settle.

Another interesting circular walk, requiring two to three hours, is to take the sunken track southwards out of Settle from Greenfoot, following the National Park boundary to Hayman Laithe to join a path, marked by stiles, below Cleatop Wood to Mearbeck Farm. From here climb up to the metalled track over Hunter Bark, which offers splendid views across Ribblesdale, before descending to Long Preston – where there are pubs, shops, and buses back to Settle. There is a choice of paths; the best, perhaps, fording the stream via Brookgill Beck and along Langber Lane to Scaleber Force, a beautiful little waterfall on Scaleber Beck, before taking the track, Lambert Lane, by Preston's Barn, and a thoroughly satisfying field path cutting past Settle Reservoir which leads directly into upper Settle.

There is also a very pleasant afternoon stroll from Settle to the historic Ebb and Flowing Well at Giggleswick. A riverside path downstream from Settle Bridge leads into Giggleswick village, from where you can walk through the attractive and historic village along Moor Lane to pick up the footpath directly across the golf course, parallel with the main road over Buckhaw Brow, over what used to be Giggleswick Tarn until it was drained last century. An Iron Age dug-out canoe was discovered on the bed of the ancient lake and sent to the supposed safety of Leeds Museum where, unfortunately, one of Hitler's bombs destroyed it in the blitz.

Where the path meets the farm track go up to the main road and almost directly across the road, in a stone trough, is the Ebb and Flowing Well.

This little curiosity was once highly regarded as a major tourist attraction; but then in former years, before the modern road was built, the waters of the well flowed spectacularly across the road rather, than now, simply rising about four or five inches in their stone prison. The well really does work, best on a dry morning after a night's heavy rain, though you often wait in vain to see any movement. Its action is probably the result of a complex syphoning effect of subterranean chambers.

Unless you want to walk up a busy and frankly unpleasant main road, return back along the same path where, at Moor Road, instead of going back through the village you can take the footpath on the immediate right-hand side of the quarry (signposted) which crosses the high land above the quarry, offering splendid views across Ribblesdale and Pen y Ghent. There is a choice of ways back to Settle, the simplest being to pick up the track through Lord Wood which emerges on a quiet estate road and the main road west of Settle Bridge.

But for a surprisingly lovely extension to this walk, follow the footpath which has been diverted round the outside of the quarry edge to pick up an ancient, sunken path, marked by stiles, through the bracken along the top of Giggleswick Scar. This passes Schoolboy Tower where many a schoolboy from Giggleswick School, willingly or otherwise, has panted up, and along a limestone terrace offering views right across and along the top of

Buckhaw Brow, and, as you climb the summit, westwards towards the majestic fells of Bowland and on towards the Lake District. From Buckhaw Brow top the path joins the bridleway, northwards, to Feizor, but you can return to Settle by picking up the footpath that climbs back over the top to Stackhouse and the riverside path to Settle.

Giggleswick itself is a quiet and totally unexpected village, tucked away from the roar of traffic on the main road, with its seventeenth-century cottages and houses, the stream through the centre of the village and its ancient church. There are some quite delightful paths to discover, particularly if you are arriving at the railway station (regular service, weekdays and summer Sundays, on the Leeds–Morecambe line) and heading towards the limestone scars. Take the path, for instance, which runs from the road to the west of the station (avoid the temptation to use the private drive at the side of the pub; there is strictly no access along here) to Close House, and from there follow an unusual and interesting field path which goes by the green-domed school chapel to emerge at the side of the school; turn left up the lane here to locate a little path, right, that cuts across by the school observatory and offers unusual and surprising views back across Giggleswick and across the Ribble to Settle town.

To the west and south of the station paths radiate towards Eldroth and Rathmell and the high fells of Bowland; excellent walking but belonging to Bowland.

Most ramblers, indeed, will be drawn by the white crags to the north. A good route to them is to take the path from Settle Bridge, round the outside of the school playing fields following the river upstream that eventually emerges on the lane at Stackhouse. Follow the path behind Stackhouse climbing steeply up through the woods, at right angles with the slope, to locate a stile in the wall directly ahead. Avoid taking the ladder stile to the left which leads back along the ridge to Settle. Your way is directly ahead up onto the limestone clints, by a Bronze Age tumulus, bearing left, following the wall along, till, at a gate, the path changes to the other side of the wall and continues beyond a sheepfold – careful map-reading needed here – over the low ridge which offers fine views of Ingleborough, before descending into Feizor, a monastic settlement and staging point on important pack-horse routes between the north of Lancashire and Yorkshire. You can return to

Ribblesdale, indeed, along the ancient pack-horse way by taking a path that starts through a broad metal gate only a few yards north of the point where you emerge on the lane into Feizor, and following a deep sunken way along the wall side which goes through a shallow but natural pass through the ridge, with the craggy tops of Pot Scar and Smearsett Scar directly to your left, and the path falling away steeply as the way descends to Stainforth, by the Jacobean House at Knight Stainforth and the beautiful pack-horse bridge over the Ribble above Stainforth Falls. A very pleasant riverside path, clearly marked by stiles, leads back to the weir and salmon leap at Langcliffe, and on, by the riverside, to Settle.

Stainforth, easily reached from Settle by this riverside route, or by bus or by car (good car park available), is another excellent point from which to explore Ribblesdale. The village, now bypassed by main road, has a renewed quietness and charm, a shop and an old inn. If you cross the stepping-stones in the middle of the village and continue up Goat Lane, a stony track, you soon reach Catrigg Force, near the top of the lane, through a stile, left. Follow the steps down to view a majestic little fall, thin columns of water plunging down a narrow gorge, at its very best after heavy frost when spray freezes like white powder, and icicles hang like long, pale fingers. Many people believe it to be the most beautiful fall in Craven – they may well be right.

If you follow the path across and left to Winskill, keeping left through a stile before Winskill Farm and a long, undulating path above Langcliffe Quarry, it joins Howson Lane which leads directly into the centre of Langcliffe village, another little village of great prettiness, built around a large village green, with a fountain and a fine old tree on the green. Langcliffe Hall, nearby, is the most impressive house in Upper Ribblesdale, dating from the seventeenth century and with many associations with the Dawson family.

From Langcliffe follow the road across the railway before bearing off left to the river and the weir, and the riverside path back to Stainforth Bridge. Alternatively, if you are going back to Settle, do not walk along the road, but follow the lane back uphill to pick up the bridleway, right, which goes directly back to Constitution Hill, Settle.

Pen y Ghent

Pen y Ghent is one of the great mountains in England. If you do not believe me, see it on a bright, clear, cold day in the middle of winter, covered with light snow, when against the blue of the sky its very dramatic, powerful shape makes it appear as a massive Alpine peak. That is, of course, an illusion; Pen y Ghent is the smallest, indeed, of the big sisters, a lowly 2,277 feet or mere 694 metres.

But in every sense a mountain, stark, steep, and splendid, with, if you know where to look, an authentic sub-Alpine flora and a steep, shattered nose which even experienced mountaineers must cross with care. Its Celtic name suggests its associations with the Kingdom of Brigantia, and the Celtic tribes forced westwards by later invasions of Roman and Teutonic settlers until only the remotest fastnesses remained. Its name is supposed to mean Hill of the Winds – a fitting description on most days of the year.

It is not a difficult climb; the easiest route indeed is from Daleshead on the Stainforth–Halton Gill road. You can park near the cattle grid and follow the track to Churn Milk Hole, before following the Pennine Way route across the pasture to the wall side and up that impressive nose to the soft, flat summit mound, an exhilarating viewpoint, commanding the head of Littondale, Fountains Fell, Lower Ribblesdale, the Bowland Fells and the Irish Sea and, in the distance, the Lake District.

The best short day's walk is from Horton in Ribblesdale. Horton has a good car park, the excellent Pen y Ghent Café, which is a veritable hikers' mecca, offering excellent food, liquid refreshment and creature comforts most hours of the day for weary walkers, and outdoor equipment. The village also boasts a welcoming pub. Horton has lost its prettiness to the constant roar of quarry traffic, and badly needs a bypass. But once away from the roaring engines, the village takes a different flavour. Follow the little path by the old church and along the back lane to the hamlet of Brackenbottom where, just before the farm on the left, a well-signed path goes through a gate left, and alongside the wall, uphill – a very clear and obvious route, although differing from most Ordnance Survey maps because of an impending diversion. This path climbs steadily up over the limestone outcrops, with increasingly splendid views to compensate for the effort, and the massive shape of the summit ridge, a kind of gritstone sphinx, looming ever nearer. Indeed, on a grey and misty day the mountain seems to have an almost overpowering presence as you approach its gloomy face, a mysterious, even slightly sinister quality, as if recalling its ancient history. And, then, when the weather clears, all is sharpness, brilliance, magic. Who says mountains are not living things?

The way down is along the miners' path, the Pennine Way, descending an attractive terrace route, sheltered and pure bliss if the wind has been biting on the summit, soon swinging directly down the hillside over a broad and damaged surface battered by the erosion of thousands of Three Peaks walkers.

Soon after the path crosses a beck and a stile at a wall, look for a deviating path on the left to Hunt Pot, an impressive and somewhat startling chasm leading to an extensive underground pothole system. But for an even more impressive feature, where the main path reaches the little shooting hut at the top of Horton Scar Lane, follow the path up the shallow valley to Hull Pot, a truly impressive natural amphitheatre, with Hull Pot Beck forming an attractive little waterfall, depending on its level of flow, into the great ravine. You can, with care, scramble part way into the ravine, but limestone, particularly when wet, is treacherously slippy under modern rambling-boot soles and the ravine is a steep one.

Horton Scar Lane provides a pleasant, easy descent back into Horton, with views down into the dry valley of Douk Ghyll Scar and across to the silhouette of Pen y Ghent.

There are some interesting alternative routes off Pen y Ghent, particularly the Three Peaks route northwards by Jack Daw Hill. These are shown with great clarity on Arthur Gemmell's little Three Peaks Footpath Map and Guide, authoritative and invaluable for anyone exploring this region.

North of Pen y Ghent is wild, austere country, culminating in the bleak, treeless drumlins around Ribblehead, a landscape of vast, empty horizons dominated by the great rounded summit domes of the Three Peaks, and in the foreground, the Settle–Carlisle railway, its own massive dimensions dwarfed into insignificance and yet giving a human scale to the vastness of the landscape.

But this is superb walking country by any standards; a heroic landscape of elemental forces, sky, air, and land moulded into great curves and parabolas, strong, sculptured shapes. That is one reason why any mass afforestation of this unique area would be a tragedy of the highest order, a taming and a belittling of a true wilderness; why the South House Moor scheme, just across Ribblesdale from Pen y Ghent was so bitterly controversial and why, at the end of the day, the Secretary of State was right to turn the scheme down.

Yet in the bleakest stretches of country are gills of the most delicate loveliness, green and fertile around some plunging force or turbulent beck. You come upon such gills in Ribblesdale with surprising suddenness. Take for example Ling Gill, on the Pennine Way just below the ancient bridge "repaired at the expense of the entire West Riding" in 1742; it is as beautiful a little valley as can be imagined, now a nature reserve of regional importance. You look down into the gill from the Pennine Way. Or loveliest of all, Thorns Gill, carrying Gayle Beck, the major source beck of the Ribble, crossed by an ancient and incredibly lovely pack-horse bridge that surmounts a deep, peat-brown pool. This entire gill has a path along it, and if you know where to look you can find Capnut Cave, an enticing little scramble several hundred yards long.

The best way to reach Ling Gill and Thorns Gill from Horton is not the Pennine Way, excellent though that is, but to leave the Pennine Way at Sell Gill and follow the path that runs along the top of the limestone terrace and pavements by High Pasture (excellent views throughout) to Birkwith and then along the Pennine Way to look into Ling Gill. Thorns Gill can be reached from Crake Hill along a path that crosses God's Bridge, the name frequently used in the Pennines to describe a slab of limestone forming a natural bridge across a beck, continuing by Nether Lodge and Crutchin Gill to the deserted hamlet of Thorns from where a proposed new path will take you directly to the gill, or even better, you can reach the north-east of the gill at the foot-bridge behind Gearstones, before following the path to the pack-horse bridge. A path leads directly from the bridge up to the main road.

You can, with time and energy, plan splendid days in the higher fells moving northwards from Horton over the passes into Littondale or Wharfedale, via Foxup, High Greenfield to Beckermonds or, following the Pennine Way or the Dales Way back from Gearstones up to Cam Fell summit and down to Oughtershaw. The Pennine Way over Dodd Fell provides the best way into Wensleydale, and the Dales Way over Newby Fell goes into Dentdale.

There is, if you have taken care to study the relevant timetables, a summer Tuesday and Saturday tea-time bus back from Ribblehead to Horton and Settle (operated by D. W. Whaites of Settle) and on certain weekends of the year, Dales Rail trains stop at Ribblehead Station at the end of that magnificent railway viaduct for Settle, Skipton and Leeds.

The best walking route back to Horton is, however, to take the path south-west from Birkwith to cross the Ribble at the recently restored foot-bridge at Selside and to give yourself time to explore Alum Pot reached by field path (entrance fee payable at the farm) from the corner of the track that leaves the main road, north of Selside, for Clapham. Alum Pot is the most awesome of potholes, a huge, terrifying chasm swirling with spray and foam, a veritable entrance to Dante's *Inferno*. Several smaller pots nearby, Long Churn and Diccan and others offer pot-holing and caving opportunities. The small charge payable to reach the Alum Pot complex is worth it.

From Alum Pot return to the main walled track, continuing up across the high limestone pavement to Sulber Gait and up to the Three Peaks route down Sulber Nick to Horton in Ribblesdale, a right of way, recently dedicated and therefore not shown on all but the most recent Ordnance Survey maps, which follows the ancient path to Beecroft Hall and Horton. But this is on the shoulder of Pen y Ghent's most famous neighbour, Ingleborough.

Ingleborough

Ingleborough is, as a mountain walk, even more popular than Pen y Ghent. I suppose this is partially explained by the geographic proximity of the town of Ingleton, with all its many tourist attractions as well as the villages of Horton and Clapham. But also, I suspect, because it is so self-evidently a major peak, visible for so many miles around, the most dominant of the Three Peaks, standing isolated in space, a gaunt, carved-out hunk of rock. Wherever you are in the area you cannot escape it, a constant reminder and a challenge. It is easy to get at, with routes from all

sides, routes again all splendidly documented by Arthur Gemmell in his Three Peaks map. It offers a climb which even the
relatively unfit can enjoy – not too severe or too daunting, and yet
a remarkable sense of achievement when you reach the summit
cairn and windshelter with unsurpassed views from all sides of
the great summit triangle. No matter how many other people are
there when you get to the summit (and its popularity is in the
Scafell and Helvellyn class – you can go up at midnight in the
middle of November and find people up there, or so it seems)
Ingleborough never disappoints and always offers that marvellous sense of renewing an old and trusted acquaintance when
you reach the top.

It is, of course, geologically fascinating. You can see all the
layers of the great layer-cake as you climb, the ancient Silurian
slates around its southern skirt, the Great Scar limestones, the
alternating shales, sandstones and Yoredale limestones that
seem to continue right to the summit, the shake holes, caverns
and dry gorges where glaciers and melt-waters have carved weird
features, the occasional huge erratic boulders carried by the ice,
and the final gritstone cap, dark and menacing, on the strangely
flat summit plateau.

This plateau contains of course that great hill-fort site of the
Iron Age Brigantes, and you can trace out the hut circles even yet
in the peat and sand of the summit, and marvel how, even in the
warmer climate of Romano-British times, a community could
have survived in these bleak conditions.

The least satisfying way of climbing Ingleborough is undoubtedly the one that most people take, from Ingleton up the
stony lane and track from Storrs Common, Fell Lane, past Crina
Bottom Farm. This is a slow, rather dullish slog, fairly steady
going until the last murderous haul onto the summit plateau. The
best, I believe, is from Clapham, if for no other reason than you
can enjoy a walk through the beautifully landscaped grounds of
Ingleborough Estate (small entrance fee payable – this forms part
of the Reginald Farrer Trail) to rejoin the right of way through
Trow Gill, another of those steep and narrowly enclosed limestone gorges, before climbing up above the limestones and crossing by Bar Pot to Gaping Gill, that huge underground cavern
which, for its size (they say you could place St Paul's Cathedral
inside) and its superb underground waterfall, the highest in

England, is one of the wonders of Yorkshire. Incidentally, go along on a Bank Holiday and local caving groups will offer you a trip down on a specially rigged chair lift. As they point out with typical laconic Dales wit, "it costs nowt to go down, you only pay for the ride back up again".

From Gaping Gill the path climbs directly up Little Ingleborough to the first cairn, an exceedingly steep climb, but not difficult if you take your time, from there ascending more gently to the summit ridge immediately to the north before traversing round by the remnants of Iron Age walls (difficult to determine what is natural scree and what is man-made) for the summit.

You can, of course, follow the Crina Bottom route back to Ingleton, and though a dull ascent it makes a very pleasant descent; you get the tricky sections over first, scrambling over a boulder field and thereafter all is simple, gentle descent with time to enjoy the view. But if you need to get back to Clapham for a parked vehicle or the evening train from Clapham Station, head almost due south from Little Ingleborough cairn towards Newby Cote. There is no sign of a path on the ground until you approach Newby and pick up old sledge tracks by the old quarry. The hamlet provides an easy bearing in good conditions; in mist careful use of a compass is required if you are not to go badly wrong in a place of few landmarks. From Newby a quiet lane, or parallel ancient, sunken green way – Laithbutts Lane – leads to Clapham village.

From Horton the route is the Three Peaks walk from Horton Station and Brackenbottom, along the Iron Age path known as Sulber Nick, a deep sunken way eroded into the limestone. Follow it right up, past the shooting hut, onto the shoulder of Simon Fell and a lovely traverse on the great saddle between Ingleborough and Simon Fell to the summit. The Three Peaks route from the Hill Inn, Chapel le Dale, needs a little care; here current Ordnance Survey maps show a bridleway running over The Arks, a highly dangerous place to descend, dangerous enough on foot let alone on horseback, with a near vertical slope. The more sensible route, used by most walkers, is to the east, running through the becks to the east of the wall across Humphrey Bottom, or alternatively, and favoured by many walkers, along the wall further to the east on Simon Fell.

Finally, a great ridge walk can be achieved along the entire

Ingleborough massif to or from Ribblehead. From the footpath which runs over Gauber High Pasture at Ribblehead, between Salt Lake cottages and the Ingleton road at Chapel le Dale, a path can be traced following the wall from Colt Park, keeping immediately to the north-west side of the wall up Park Fell, and onto the Simon Fell ridge, traversing the north shoulder of Simon Fell to a stile, the Simon Fell saddle and the Ingleborough summit ridge. Complete this by a descent to Clapham, Ingleton or Horton and you have completed one of the great ridge walks of the Pennines. Again, Arthur Gemmell's map is essential here.

The skirts of Ingleborough, particularly around Clapham and Austwick, offer some fine walking. From Clapham do not fail to take the path that leads off Thwaite Lane, between Clapham and Austwick, up to Norber Scar, to see the strange Silurian erratics, great, grey, boulders, huge objects perched strangely on top of the limestone pavements left, like stranded whales by retreating glaciers millennia ago. In places further weathering and eroding of the limestone has left strange toadstools of white rock, protected from the elements, upon which the Silurian boulders perch. Few places give a more dramatic sense of the massive effects of glaciation and of man's true insignificance. The boulders were placed where we see them before western civilization as we know it began.

An attractive field path to the south offers an alternative route from Austwick to Clapham, but both villages are excellent starting-points for rambles into Crummackdale, one of the most fascinating and beautiful of all the limestone dales.

From Clapham, for example, Ling Lane, which leaves Thwaite Lane just a short distance beyond the tunnels under the Ingleborough Estate gardens, is, in fact, an ancient road which strikes high across a natural pass through the limestone, Sulber Gate for Selside and Alum Pot. This track has a connecting bridleway dropping down Crummack to the farm, but better to keep your height up onto Thieves Moss and to take the path that climbs over the very lip of the great dale head, over Beggars' Stile (an intriguing name) down to Hammer Knot and Crummack Farm for Austwick.

From Austwick another way climbs up over Norber Brow to Copple Bank and Moughton Scar high onto the limestone pavement where the junipers grow, following the quarry fence round to join the Sulber path for Horton.

This same track can be reached from a lovely complex of green tracks and paths from the Wharfe and Feizor areas – one branch of the lane from Wharfe, a beautiful, ancient hamlet, crosses a little ford to join the main track from Austwick for Crummack, the other, contouring round becomes the main track, Moughton Lane, for Horton.

All are beautiful, quiet tracks, offering a variety of views onto high limestone crags and pavements, their startling whiteness constantly making the summits look very much higher and more remote than they in actuality are. They connect, too, with other historic paths for example around the edge of Wharfe Wood to Feizor and back over to Stainforth and Settle, that are as rich in contrasting beauty. It is an exciting, unusual area with much to offer.

Further to the east, and dominating the area between Austwick and Horton, are the great Ribblesdale quarries. One path, indeed, from Newfield House, scrambles right up through and past the entire complex around Dry Rigg and Foredale.

Quarries do not improve the landscape. They create wealth and they create jobs and in the age in which we live only the most romantic and naïve would wish they were not there. In fact there are, for the geologically minded, some splendid exposures of the twisted beds of Silurian slates which, among the great, exposed faces and excavations have a kind of raw beauty. The tiny hamlet of Foredale, really a row of quarrymen's cottages perched incongruously on a green slope between the great craters, seems to defy gravity. Maybe this is not your kind of scenery; so be it. But they are a necessary reminder that the Dales are, in the final analysis, as much a part of industrial civilization as the motor car or train that carries us there; and to imagine otherwise is an illusion.

Whernside
Although the highest, Whernside is the least popular and perhaps the least known of the Three Peaks. It is, of course, the least accessible, not having any villages immediately under its shadow, Ribblehead hardly being a metropolis. It is more immediately associated with a range of hills of similar scale, Gre-

gareth, Rise Hill, Great Coum, Baugh Fell, to a degree that despite its height, it does not dominate the countryside in the manner of Pen y Ghent and Ingleborough. Except from Ribblehead and perhaps the Kingsdale road you are not even aware that it is there, or if you do notice its long, gentle silhouette it does not occur to you that you are looking at the highest peak in the Dales. But it is there, and a splendid mountain to climb.

Do not climb it by the Three Peaks route, a nasty scree slope, eroded into the hillside above Winterscales. This has nothing to recommend it except shortness, and that is no reason for climbing a mountain. A far better route is to follow the old Craven Way from Ribblehead Viaduct which goes alongside the arches and the railway line, past Blea Moor sidings and signal-box, over the double bridge over the railway line which is also an aqueduct for Force Gill, leaving the Craven Way to climb up Force Gill and visit the beautiful little waterfall, hidden in its own quiet ravine – a place to stand and marvel at the exquisite beauty of water, rock, small trees and grasses, in primrose time like a perfect hanging garden.

The path climbs round the fence above Force Gill, above Greensett Crags and steeply up to the summit ridge by Greensett Tarn, continuing up to the high trig. point, with as you would expect a splendid view across to Ingleborough, the Lakeland Hills, Morecambe Bay and many of the northern summits. Particularly impressive is the tiny railway viaduct below you, with if you are lucky, an Inter-City express dwarfed into insignificance.

The best way down to Ribblehead is to descend the series of gigantic steps off the summit, continuing along the ridge to the cairn at Low Pike, then bearing south along the Three Peaks down to Bruntscar, and the bridleway by Ivescar and Gunnerfleet to the viaduct.

An even better way off the mountain is to continue along the ridge, gradually losing height until your route merges with Kirkby Gate, an ancient bridleway from Ribblehead down to Ingleton, a thrilling descent through a natural limestone "nick" zigzagging through Twisleton Scars to Twisleton Lane and either path through the waterfalls back to Ingleton.

Equally fine, perhaps, and a classic walk of the Pennines if and when transport can be arranged (Dales Rail provides the perfect opportunity) is to tackle the mountain from Dent, picking up the

Craven Way track above Whernside Manor, along that lovely, perfect green way terracing around the northern slopes of the mountain past the point where the enclosure ends at Boot of the Wold to follow the wall up, keeping ahead for the Pike, a tall cairn, on the end of the ridge. From the Pike you climb up to the strange tarns, still, shallow pools in the middle of the bleak moorland, continuing southwards to pick up, on your left, the paths to the summit ridge. This has all the elements of a highly satisfying ridge walk, views from either side, getting progressively more dramatic as you ascend and look over the brow of the mountain into the space beyond; all great walking. Those people who underrate Whernside do not know the half.

A further alternative, and perhaps the easiest option, is to tackle the summit from the Ingleton–Deepdale road leaving a vehicle at a convenient point on the unfenced stretch of road just opposite the summit, following the outside of the enclosure wall at Cable Rake for the summit ridge – a stiff and frankly relatively tedious climb.

The south-eastern slopes of Whernside, the valley of the Doe between the mountain and Ingleborough, offer much of interest and even fascination, with a good network of footpaths to explore. The most important of these is Kirkby Gate, referred to above, which derives its name from when it was the ancient road from Ingleton to Kirkby Stephen. It forms a marvellous, yet fairly easy, high-level walk to or from Ribblehead (where it forms a natural junction with the Craven Way). You can follow it without any difficulty from Ribblehead through Ivescar, Bruntscar and Ellerbeck, keeping straight ahead over the open moorland of Scales Moor to a fine area of limestone pavement culminating in the nick referred to above. There are surprisingly fine views of the Lancashire coast from this path, before the descent into Ingleton.

From this old way, paths descend to Weathercote and Chapel le Dale. Although the famous Weathercote Cave painted by Turner is now closed to the public because of a recent accident, you can easily discover Hurtle Pot just behind the church, and further up, by Winterscales Beck, the little Gatekirk Cave. Wainwright's *Walks in Limestone Country* is particularly helpful in suggesting ways of reaching these delightful and picturesque pot-holes, but do not always assume that rights of way or access exist.

Whilst at Chapel le Dale do not neglect to visit the little churchyard, described in Southey's novel *The Doctor* and where a memorial plaque commemorates over a hundred men who died of disease and epidemics during the building of the Settle–Carlisle railway.

At the very end of the great Whernside ridge, and straddling the point where the Rivers Doe and Greta meet, is the town of Ingleton, a justifiably popular centre for exploring the south-western part of the Dales. It has everything a busy little tourist centre should; picturesque streets, cafés, inns, good car parking, a good bus service (regular buses to Skipton and Lancaster, occasionally to Kirkby Lonsdale and Kendal) and a general air of welcoming the visitor. The town is dominated, in fact, by a huge, disused railway viaduct, part of the former Ingleton–Tebay railway. Now redundant, it would make a splendid walkway if only someone had the wit to cut through the bureaucratic jungle of legal responsibilities and open it up as a walkway between the town car park and community centre and Thornton in Lonsdale.

Ingleton's real claim to fame must be the waterfalls. They are, without fear of contradiction, the best in England, a series of splendid gorges and ravines, with rapids and falls hurtling through them. You can, from the main entrance at the bridge at the bottom of the town, (large car park and cafeteria at the entrance) make a splendid circular tour of some four and a half miles (allow three hours), walking up the specially engineered paths and bridges, crossing and re-crossing the falls, going through an area of great geological interest, with pre-Cambrian, Silurian and Ordovician rocks in close juxtaposition and, in places, marvellously exposed. The best way is undoubtedly to follow the Greta up first through Swilla Glen to Pecca Falls and the majestic cascade of Thornton Force, one you can, with care, scramble behind and where, in a few amazing inches, rocks of over two hundred and fifty million years difference in age can be observed along a line of unconformity.

From Thornton Force the path joins Twisleton Lane to Scar End, from where the path descends to Beezley Farm and Beezley Falls on the Doe, with Beezley Falls, Snow Falls and Twisleton Glen to delight you. There is no public right of way through the falls, and a small entrance charge (the ticket gives a simple sketch-map of the falls) is payable. You must, however, exercise extreme caution around the falls, keeping to paths and not attempting to scramble around the sides of the narrow gorges. A number of fatal accidents have occurred in recent years, particularly to youngsters who, once slipping into the narrow ravines, have little or no chance of survival. This is a popular tourist spot, but in its way as dangerous a place as anywhere in the Pennines. An added attraction from the top of the falls is to cut across the field path at Beezley direct to White Scar Cave, one of the best show caves of the Pennines, and open most days.

Away from the mountain summits and the main tourist routes, there are other pleasant walks from Ingleton to be explored – by Greenwood Leghe, Cold Cotes and Newby to Clapham, across the fields to Bentham, across the Greta to Thornton in Lonsdale and Masongill. Like so often in the Craven Dales, the contrast between the crowded tourist routes and virtually deserted other paths could not be more marked.

But one route along the Kingsdale side of Whernside should not be neglected, and that is the path from Twisleton Lane above the falls to Braida Garth, along the lane by Yordas Cave, another of the famous old show caves (permission required from Braida Garth Farm). A path can be followed from Yordas to Bull Pot, and along the ancient turbary (peat) road above the limestone scars to descend by Tow Scar and Hunt Cross to Twisleton Lane. This is a very fine walk.

The Three Peaks Walk

I confess a growing prejudice to marathon walks of any kind. They begin as a romantic challenge enjoyed by a few, become a cult enjoyed by the many, and descend to a dreary mass trek undertaken by thousands of youngsters who care neither for the country nor for the paths they follow, hate every moment of it and look forward to getting back to the comfort of home. Perhaps this is a cynical view, but countryside is to be enjoyed, relished, treasured, not suffered.

Not that you could possibly walk the Three Peaks and, at some point, however unwittingly, fail to absorb something of the grandeur of the landscape. Many people have clearly been introduced to our northern hills because of the Three Peaks Walk, and some came again. Taking a Benthamite utilitarian view, many people's lives have clearly been enriched by the experience even if under duress. Suffering, we are told, has a beneficial side. That is as may be – but the sight of young people limping along the road into Horton in Ribblesdale on almost any day of the year, and in veritable hordes on summer weekends, is, ultimately, a rather sad one. Many will never walk on the hills again, or forever associate the mountains with blisters and misery.

Like it or not the Three Peaks Walk will stay. It has become an institution, and the British cherish their institutions. Most farmers along the route agree that it has "got out of hand" and accept, philosophically, the need for a hard, well-signed path throughout the entire route along which the slowly moving army of coloured anoraks will bob leaving the rest of their fields and stock undisturbed.

Both Wainwright and Gemmell, whilst describing many alternative routes, do give you the route in detail and I have no wish to attempt to supplant them. In summary, however, start from Horton where the excellent Pen y Ghent Café will offer you a unique "clocking-in" system to record your departure and return time. Follow the Brackenbottom path to Pen y Ghent, either path via Hull Pot or Black Dub Moss past Birkwith and God's Bridge to Nether Lodge where the shortest way (heaven forbid) follows the main road to Ribblehead for Winter Scales; a far better alternative is via Thorns to Gearstones and across the edge of Blea Moor to Force Gill and Whernside summit. From here the most direct path is down Bruntscar to the Hill Inn, up from Souther Scales to Simon Fell and Ingleborough summit, before picking up the traverse to Sulber Nick and back to Horton via Beecroft. The most direct route involving some frankly nasty road walking is twenty-two miles, the very much better route via Thorns is twenty-three. Work out for yourself the thousands of feet or metres climbed if these things are important to you.

Less attractive are the massive scars on the landscape the non-stop procession of feet has caused, and the creeping erosion in wet areas and bogs where each new band of walkers veers to the left or right to avoid the black and foul mud, thus encroaching on virgin areas. It can be particularly bad after a wet spring before the new grass has time to be established.

It is a serious problem. The authorities have, as always, responded with effort that is too little and too late. Unless something is done soon, the Three Peaks Walk will become a minor environmental disaster, ripping off the surface vegetation from square miles of mountainside. It can, of course, recover, and scars will heal, but not until a firm, engineered path has been built over the vulnerable parts of the route. Purists may raise their collective hands in horror at the thought but, unless there is to be a major change in leisure habits or the Three Peaks Walk formally closed – an unthinkable prospect – there is no alternative.

REFERENCE

Maps
Ordnance Survey Landranger 1:50,000 Sheet 104 Wensleydale and Wharfedale
Ordnance Survey Outdoor Leisure 1:25,000 The Three Peaks
Three Peaks Footpaths Map and Guide, Arthur Gemmell (Stile Maps)

Books
Walks in Limestone Country, A. Wainwright (Westmorland Gazette, 1970)
Walking in the Craven Dales, Colin Speakman (Dalesman, 1973)
Walking in the Three Peaks, Colin Speakman (Dalesman, 1983)

7

Dentdale

I confess a special partiality for Dentdale. It has a very distinctive personality of its own, looking westwards towards the Cumbrian mountains, protected on all sides by hills not only from the worst of the weather, but also from too many tourists because it is a long way to Dentdale from almost any large centre of population. For it is cut off from Lancashire and West Yorkshire by miles of tortuous roads and from Cumbria by the Lake District. Only the M6 has recently allowed the more adventurous to turn off north of Killington to Sedbergh to find the winding road into Dent, or from Kirkby Lonsdale climbing over the narrow Barbon Pass. May Dentdale, with its delicate, intimate, and totally unspoiled beauty long be preserved from the excesses of tourism or the developer's hand.

The real way to reach Dentdale, if not on foot, is by rail, to Dent Station, the highest main-line station in England on the Settle–Carlisle railway, now open for Dales Rail services only. Passengers on the Leeds–Carlisle expresses and on Dales Rail have, in fact, perhaps the most splendid view from a railway carriage window in England as from a height of 1,100 feet they gaze down the green and fertile valley winding round to the massive outline of the distant Howgill Fells. Conversely, walkers in the valley below look up to see to their astonishment a full-scale Inter-City express seemingly floating across the side of the fell high above them, a *trompe-l'oeil* that turns out, on closer inspection, to be reality.

And it is fitting that Dentdale should be reached in such epic style; the old joke that the station was built three and a half miles from Dent Town "''appen that's where the railway was" was no joke if you were carrying luggage to the village, but sheer bliss if you have time and energy to explore the intimate linking field and riverside paths from Dent Station down the valley to the town; the more obvious route from Lea Yeat by the river to Ewegales, Little Town, Clint and the riverside being both the Dales Way and a popular route for Dales Rail walkers.

Like many of the higher and western Dales, Dentdale was a Viking settlement, occupied by raiders from the ancient Dublin kingdom of the Norsemen in the ninth century, and the present settlement pattern after all these long centuries, still reflects the pattern of scattered, isolated homesteads, rather than the nucleated settlements of the more Anglian dales to the east. Many of the farms, situated in steep little gills or on springs on the hillside keep names with a strong Norse flavour – Harber Gill, Hacker Gill, Clint, Swarthwaite, Sikeland – and the paths that connect them date from that remote period when the primeval forest and scrub were first cleared, and the yeomen farmers or Statesmen (freeholders) of Dentdale began a long tradition of husbandry of the land and self-sufficiency that lasted well into the nineteenth century. See how the enclosure walls of Dentdale, steep up the fellside, reflect a sharing out of the higher grazings to reflect the little valley holdings.

Dent was the only town of this "mountain republic" of Dentdale, and its character and individuality have, so far, survived the ravages of the twentieth century, with its marvellous cobbled main street, and its tall cottages, now lacking their high galleries where the hand knitters would work during the summer months. Not surprising the village is now an Outstanding Conservation Area – if such modern-day bureaucratic terms really mean anything.

The huge slab of Shap granite, forming a drinking-fountain in the centre of the village, is inscribed in powerful Gothic script with the name Adam Sedgwick. Sedgwick, 1785–1873, was one of the world's great geologists, a great teacher and a great Dalesman who, during his fifty-five years as Woodwardian Professor of Geology at Cambridge never forgot nor neglected his native Dentdale. Sedgwick's pamphlet *Memorial by the Trustees of Cowgill Chapel* and its subsequent *Supplement*, remain one of the most fascinating accounts of life in Dentdale before the Industrial Revolution caused a decline from which the little community has never fully recovered; even in modern Dentdale too many cottages are merely weekend homes or holiday cottages, tenanted in

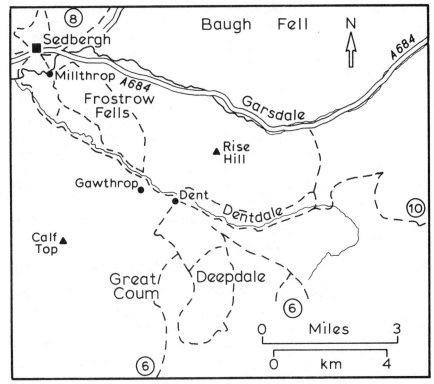

DENTDALE

the summer, empty in the winter. The once busy industries have ceased, the old communities dispersed. Whether or not tourism can be used to help create a revival of economic activity in Dentdale is still an open question.

Dent is, in fact, an excellent walking centre, with opportunity for several days' varied and interesting rambling in the immediate vicinity of the town and farther afield. Pubs, cafés, shops and a large car park make it easy for the motorized walker to enjoy a day's walk without undue difficulty. Bus services are, however, virtually non-existent, with a Wednesday market day bus only (to Kendal) and a service to Dent Station on Dales Rail days. Otherwise you must rely on taxis or, if you can afford the time, take advantage of farmhouse and guest-house accommodation in and around the village. There is a youth hostel at Denthead. A warm welcome to unattached walkers is always extended at Whernside

Cave and Fell Centre, on the back road a mile from Dent. Whernside Centre, of course, offers a number of fell walking and special interest courses that provide perhaps the finest way of all to discover the real Dentdale – see Chapter Two.

Perhaps the most popular walk from Dent begins from the south of the village, behind the main street where there is a village green. Follow the road past the vicarage which soon becomes a track climbing steeply uphill up Flintergill, an attractive wooded glade with views back across the roof-tops of Dent and to Rise Hill behind. The track climbs steeply through a gate to join a high-level track, the Occupation Road. Follow it left, contouring round the fell below Great Coum, a marvellous high-level track with panoramic views across and up the dale. At the first junction the track that descends is Nun House Outrake ("outrake" – a fine piece of Norse compression signifying hill track leading to the top land); follow it down to Nun House Farm, and then the waymarked path through to the road above Mill Bridge, site of the old Deepdale Mill. From Mill Bridge a busy riverside path loops by Deepdale Beck and the River Dee back to Dent, with an alternative more direct though slightly less obvious path which runs past Double Cross and along the old mill-race to Church Bridge below Dent.

The walk can be extended by continuing along the Occupation Road beyond Nun House Outrake, curving right under Great Coum before the track swings under old quarries and down to the Deepdale Road, not far from the summit over Kingsdale. A field path begins at a stile above White Shaw by Mire Garth and Brightholme, bearing left to join the track to Whernside Manor and the mill bridge path back to Dent. This is a lovely walk, never better than in late spring when the wild flowers are in abundance, particularly when the hedgerows are creamy white with the froth of blackthorn.

Dentdale is unusual in the Dales in that it is a marvellous dale for hedgerows; the milder, gentler climate seems to allow these hedges to break into bud earlier, and more lushly than they do in the predominantly dry-stone Dales to the east. Dentdale has something of the greener, richer vegetation of the Lake District so that even a walk, for example, along the back lane between the village and Lea Yeat, or up to Denthead is pure magic when the spring flowers struggle into early life. The river, too, is a strange, fascinating river, disappearing completely in places when the water-table is low, creating deep gorges and chasm at certain places like the legendary Hell's Cauldron, then resurging into a raging torrent.

Another popular walk is simply to follow the Dales Way back from Dent Town to Lea Yeat, and then to trace the path back along the north side of the valley past Cowgill, Spice Gill, Blands, along the lane to Bank Lands and along the hillside to Scotchergill and Hall Bank. Careful path finding is required; no verbal description can do it justice, and you require Three Peaks Outdoor Leisure 1:25,000 or the Dales Way Footpath Map and Guide by Arthur Gemmell which includes Dentdale paths. This is not a walk to hurry, with stiles to find and gates to open (and close). Waymarking has very much improved in recent years but there are still gaps.

North of Dent a very pleasant long afternoon's walk can be taken by following the river either from Church Bridge or where the riverside path meets the road north-west of the village to Barth Bridge and continuing along beyond Dillicar to join the quiet back lane to Rash Bridge (the ford at Brackensgill is too deep to cross in comfort) and the lovely Rash Mill, a historic water-mill being restored by the boys of Sedbergh School. Cross Rash Bridge, turning back up the main road to Dent before finding a signposted path – the Dales Way again – that climbs up to the pasture to join the green way between Dent and Sedbergh by Millthrop. This does, in fact, form a superb walk from Dent, with a magnificent view across the great bowl in the fells that contains Sedbergh. But if you are returning to Dent, follow the path that bears off by stiles beyond Gap Farm to Burton Hill, a beautiful little Jacobean farmstead down to the main road at Craggs Hill. A short way along the road, at Mire House, a path leads directly to the riverside and Barth Bridge.

For longer walks, if there is more time available, there are several extremely pleasant and varied routes between Dent and Sedbergh, all clearly shown on the Sedbergh Footpath Map prepared for the National Park Committee by Arthur Gemmell in 1977. One simple but very delightful one is to continue along the Rash Mill road which winds through the narrow gorge formed by the River Dee as it bursts through the main terminal moraine at the bottom of the valley before joining the Rawthey. A path from a stile, right, where the road bends left, follows the river round, delightfully, to Abbot Holme Bridge, going behind Cat Holes (where the farmer operates one of the bunkhouse barns from a converted barn behind the farm), from where another stile, left, leads to a field path up the little hillock with the delightful name of Elysian Fields and the foot-bridge at Birks for Sedbergh.

From Sedbergh you might return along the bridleway from Millthrop, the Dales Way, and then via Burton Hill as referred to above, or, for a more strenuous walk, take the high-level path along the top of the golf course, or perhaps one of several attractive paths via High Side, to pick up the old green way via Hollins onto the Frostrow Fells, climbing up above Longstone (the old green road is marginally better than the parallel footpath) to Long Moor top and down the track to Lunds and Hollow House. This is a particularly interesting route because for a good part of the way it follows the Dent Fault, that major geological split between the Carboniferous rocks of the Yorkshire Dales and the older Silurian rocks of the Lake District. Geologists will be able to trace out the evidence of the fault line and the complex breccias frequently exposed in stream beds where the two systems meet.

Dentdale offers marvellous opportunities for longer days' fell walking, preferably when public transport opportunities are available (the Dales Rail train and bus service in effect open up most of the longer walks from Dentdale) or if the rambler is able to stay overnight at hostel or guest-house.

A classic walk from Dent village, or Dent railway station, is to climb up the Coal Road from Lea Yeat, past the station, high up to the 1,700-foot contour line to join a broad, stony track, Galloway Gate, used by Scottish drovers up until the nineteenth century bringing cattle from the southern Scottish uplands to the markets of Craven, staying overnight at Gearstones, where there was an important drovers' inn. Galloway Gate eventually joins the old road from Artengill to Widdale high on Cross Wold, an ancient pass from Dentdale over to Hawes. It is a very satisfying tramp to follow the track over the watershed, into Widdale to Widdale Foot (although shown as a dotted line on the Ordnance map, it is in fact a county road). You must follow the B6265 for just under a mile towards Hawes, before picking up the bridleway with a foot-bridge over Widdale Beck, that climbs up Appersett Pasture for Appersett and Hawes.

From the top of Artengill, where the track is unenclosed, it is only a short climb to the summit of Great Knoutberry (2,205 feet) a superb viewpoint and well worth the effort. No formal path or access exists however.

An alternative route, and one which can be used to make a circular walk back to Dent, is to descend Artengill underneath the magnificent railway viaduct on the Settle–Carlisle line, built partly out of black limestone or "Dent marble" on the site of an old Dent marble quarry and works. Dent marble was highly prized in the last century for interior decorative purposes, making highly polished mantelpieces and even (as in Ingleborough Hall, Clapham) ornamental columns, with the fossil crinoids in the polished rock emerging with great beauty. Dent marble is really only a limestone with a high carbon content, and is fairly common locally – look at some of the stone in the bed of the Dee. The astonishing thing is that it should have gone out of fashion at all.

From Artengill and Stone House walk up the lane which skirts the edge of the infant Dee, past Denthead Youth Hostel to the bridge, right over the river at Studley Garth that leads to a fairly well-defined path to Dent Head Farm and up the side of the entrance to Blea Moor tunnel before climbing up through the forestry plantation high onto Blea Moor and along the line of Blea Moor tunnel, still marked by evidence of the workings and tunnel air shafts. The huge spoil heaps, only partially covered after a century, give vivid insight into the astonishing scale of the earthworks required to build this 2,629 yard long tunnel. Each of the air shafts you pass is ten feet in diameter, and they are 390 feet, 358 feet and 217 feet deep respectively as you pass them.

The path descends the desolate fell at Blea Moor sidings. Directly ahead is the great Ribblehead Viaduct and radiating paths to the south; but to return to Dentdale the best route is undoubtedly the Craven Way, which you can join at the aqueduct over the railway north of Blea Moor signal-box, climbing up the fell behind Force Gill and up to Hagg Worm Haw (Hagg Worms are adders) and along that marvellous terraced green way into D ntdale referred to in the previous chapter. It is, of course, perfectly possible to combine this walk with an ascent of Whernside.

Another thrilling way out of Dentdale is to pick up the old drovers' road out of Cowgill, that zigzags up the side of Cowgill before becoming an open fell path on the top of Black Hill. This is, in fact, one of the few official routes over Rise Hill, the long, narrow ridge between Garsdale and Dentdale. It is perfectly possible to walk the length of that ridge from Frostrow to Black Hill virtually without climbing a single wall; but no formal access exists. The old drove-road descends over the open fell on the west of Blea Gill to Dandra Garth. Like the Widdale road, this is only a black dotted line on Ordnance maps even though it is an ancient road or byway. It is always a point of some confusion that these old ways, which may or may not even have vehicular rights, are not shown by the conventional footpath or bridleway notation, though the pedestrian has every right to use them.

To the south of Dent is that magnificent and little known peak Great Coum. The best way onto it is to climb up Flintergill from Dent and then onto the Occupation Road, picking up the track to the west known as Wideron Gate that climbs to a gate into a huge open pasture, Crag Side. No formal access provision here, but well-behaved walkers have gone here for years. The summit of Great Coum is directly ahead above Crag Side, at a cairn. It is a splendid viewpoint, looking directly down at Dentdale and Deepdale. From here a descent can be made down the saddle of the fells to the great County Stone, a primeval boulder where the old counties of Lancashire, West Riding and Westmorland used to meet (West Riding and Westmorland having now been replaced by Cumbria), from where you can descend directly down to a gate leading into the Occupation Road and go either by Nun House Outrake or Deepdale back to Dent. But for the dedicated fell walker, who has planned his day with care, Gragareth awaits. From the County Stone, keep on the west side of the wall to miss the crossing walls and follow this quite stupendous ridge, over Green Hill and the long ascent of Gragareth, to the trig. station at 2,057 feet – a fine viewpoint over the Lune Valley and Lakeland hills.

From the summit of Gragareth you can either head due west to those strange, tall cairns, the Three Men of Gragareth, descending to Leck Fell House and the lane to either Leck or Ireby, or follow the boundary wall down to Over Hall for Ireby.

Wainwright's *Walks in Limestone Country* is easily the most useful guidebook for this rather tricky country where conventional maps, especially the 1:50,000, are not that helpful.

These western fells of the Dales offer, in fact, some of the most spectacular viewpoints of any fells in the Pennines, commanding as they do open vistas right up to and including the coastline which, on a clear day, can be seen in extraordinary detail, including the sands of Morecambe Bay and the Kent Estuary, Arnside Knott and the coast of Furness, and always, a dominant feature, the Lakeland peaks. It is surprising, too, from how many fell tops Blackpool Tower is a clear and distinct feature.

Strangely enough, one of the most majestic of all the fells overlooking Dentdale, with superlative views of the coast, is virtually inaccessible from Dentdale itself, and has to be approached from Barbondale or from Sedbergh. We will therefore leave it to another chapter.

REFERENCE

Maps
Ordnance Survey Landranger 1:50,000 Sheet 98 Wensleydale and
    Wharfedale
Ordnance Survey Outdoor Leisure 1:25,000 The Three Peaks
The Sedbergh Footpath Map, Arthur Gemmell (Stile Maps)
The Dales Way Footpath Map, Arthur Gemmell and Colin Speak-
    man (Stile Maps)

Books
Walks in Limestone Country, W. A. Wainwright (Westmorland
    Gazette, 1970)
Walks for Motorists in the Yorkshire Dales, Ramblers' Association
    (Warne, 1980)
Adam Sedgwick, Geologist & Dalesman, Colin Speakman (Broadoak
    Press, 1981)
Discovering Upper Dentdale, David Boulton (D. & A. Boulton,
    Sedbergh, 1984)

8

Lonsdale, the Howgill Fells
and Mallerstang

In his extreme old age, Adam Sedgwick, the great geologist and Dalesman, recalled as a schoolboy climbing up the round-topped Firbank Fells, north-west of Sedbergh, and looking down into the great basin formed by the fells and the four valleys that meet in this bowl of the hills and escape down the lovely valley of the Lune. "Should this note" he wrote, "reach the sight of any of my younger countrymen or countrywomen, I exhort them to walk to the top of one of these Firbank Fells (a very easy task), and warm their hearts by gazing over this cluster of noble Dales, among which Providence placed the land of their Fathers, and the home of their childhood."

Nothing has changed since Sedgwick wrote those words in 1870 to make them any less true or convincing. "Noble" dales, indeed, and noble fells between them, a countryside of extraordinary grandeur and beauty, and because of its geographic isolation relatively little known except for the millions speeding by on the M6 or the West Coast Main-line Railway (Euston-Glasgow) passing through the Lune Gorge who look up perhaps in wonder at the huge bulk of the Howgill Fells which suddenly fills the windscreen or carriage window.

The Howgill Fells, inevitably, dominate this part of the Dales, but it seems only logical to take the whole of Lonsdale from Tebay down to Kirkby Lonsdale, flanking as it does the Howgill massif to the west and by the same criteria to include with it that high fell country to the north and east which contains Baugh Fell, Wild Boar Fell, Mallerstang and the source of the Eden, within the same section, a semicircle of fine fell country. Drive along the road from Kirkby Lonsdale to Sedbergh and on to Kirkby Stephen and you will cross through this country, walking country of excellence. The very splendour of the landscape underlines the

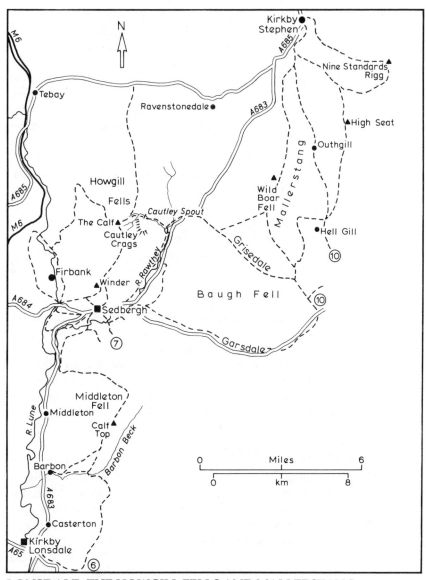

LONSDALE, THE HOWGILL FELLS AND MALLERSTANG

stupidity of local government boundaries that deem most of this area to be outside the highest categories of landscape protection – National Park status – simply because of the historic boundaries and administrative convenience. Mercifully the landscape quality owes nothing to labels placed upon it by planning officers; these western fells offer some of the very best fell walking in Britain, and if you enjoy high, open landscapes, solitude and a sense of man's insignificance, this area is beyond compare. Nor is there risk of even words like these changing the situation. There are no Three Peaks or Lyke Wake Walks here, no attractions for multitudes; if anything the area is underused, it needs more visitors, more walkers on the paths. But no shame in being élitist; solitude and wilderness are not for everyone. There will always be queues to get over Striding Edge on Helvellyn, and a procession of people up the Crina track to Ingleborough for the foreseeable future, even if a few more seekers after wilderness face the wastes of Wild Boar Fell or the emptiness of Middleton Fell. Man is, be it noted, a gregarious creature and there are a good few thousand acres of fell side still available for those who want occasionally to escape their fellow creatures.

Lonsdale
Sedbergh is not actually in Lonsdale, even though the River Lune, following one of Sedgwick's four valleys, skirts the town. Of the others, the Rawthey and the Clough curve below the town and the Dee comes in from the south at Abbot Holme. But the town provides an admirable centre not only for the immediately proximate Howgill Fells, but to explore the network of paths around the town itself and into the Lune Gorge. It does provide the best way onto the Middleton Fell range and the area around Barbon is within easy access.

The town itself is in a quite superb setting, a thrilling back-cloth of high fells, the green, rounded domes of the Howgills giving an impression of mountain grandeur that few towns in Britain can surpass. If the town itself is quiet, unspectacular, even a little dull, because unlike for example nearby Dent, it has not yet been discovered by sophisticated and the trendy, it is still very much a working community, folk who identify strongly still with the Yorkshire Dales though their links with Kendal and Cumbria have grown since 1974. It has good cafés, pubs and two large car parks, but do not expect too many souvenir or craft shops. Public transport is limited from the walker's viewpoint, being an irregular service to and from Kendal that does not operate back to Kendal on Saturday afternoons or at all on Sundays. There is a twice weekly market day bus across to Hawes and an irregular bus to Kirkby Lonsdale, but once again the Dales Rail service with its connecting buses to and from Garsdale Station opens up the area for people without their own transport on the weekends it operates. There is a National Park Information Centre at the Joss Lane car park, a converted eighteenth-century shop – once a shop selling woollen goods where George Bernard Shaw regularly purchased his socks – which now has useful local information including the Sedbergh and Howgills Footpath Maps.

It is also another good centre to make a base for a longer walking holiday, especially if you want a centre which is virtually untouched by the more predictable aspects of tourism and where, even in the height of the summer season, there will not be too many other people around. Even without a car, the range of walks you can do from Sedbergh itself is remarkably good, with the Howgills on your very doorstep, and if you are prepared to study the Ribble bus timetable carefully and plan your walks to take advantage of the buses when they do operate – for example to Garsdale Head, Dent and Kirkby Lonsdale – it is amazing how many of the longer walks in this section are within your reach. There is also a good choice of extremely reasonably priced accommodation in the town.

A popular walk lasting little more than a couple of hours from Sedbergh is to take the path behind the parish church that crosses the grounds of Sedbergh's famous public school where Adam Sedgwick was only one of many famous scholars, and the poet Hartley Coleridge – son of Samuel Taylor Coleridge – was a schoolmaster until dismissed for drunkenness. The path eventually emerges at the lane above Birks, where a further signposted path on the right crosses the fields and the old railway line to Brigflatts, where there is a little Quaker meeting-house, dating from 1675 and the early years of the Friends. The meeting-house is usually open to those respecting its quietness and its purpose, and the story of how it was built, by the Friends themselves in those years of persecution, in an area full of many associations with Quakerism and the teachings of George Fox, gives the beautiful little building and its surroundings an extraordinary significance.

From Brigflatts go up to the main road, following it westwards with care to pick up the riverside path, the "Rawthey Way", which leads along a quite enchanting section of the Dales Way, past the confluence of the Dee and the Rawthey, past Birks Mill (some magnificent exposures of Ordovician slates below the foot-bridge to interest geologists) and onto Millthrop Bridge. Turn left towards Sedbergh, but look for a stile, right, that leads to a field path across the school playing-fields into Sedbergh.

This walk can be extended by following the Dales Way further westwards through High Oaks Farm, but then following the path along the lane to the north of the farm right to the Lune and the Killington Bridge Access Area – a section of riverside now official-ly open to the public as a riverside area and forming a steep and rocky gorge with deep pool, again where the older Ordovician slates are marvellously exposed. You can return to Sedbergh either by the bridleway or field path through Ingmire Park, perhaps climbing up through Underwinder Farm to Howgill Lane to avoid walking along the very busy and dangerous A684.

East of Sedbergh the Rawthey Way can be followed up to Straight Bridge either returning by Stone Hall and Underbank – pleasant but unspectacular field paths – or better still by crossing by Fairfield Mills across the A684 and up to Hollins, following the path from Bank Cottage up to High Side Farm, a derelict farm once known as "Little Africa" because it was miles away from anywhere, with a path up above the golf course and its splendid views before descending to Millthrop Bridge. A shorter route is to follow the very pleasant path virtually along the stream via Blandses to Millthrop but expect some mud at certain times of the year.

With more time available, follow the River Clough up from Farfield and Hall Bank below the lovely Dovecot Gill with its remarkable cave (no access except with the farmer's permission) to Garsdale Foot, crossing the Clough at Danny Bridge before ascending Longstone Fell, and returning along the old green way over the Frostrow Fells. From all these paths you enjoy magnifi-cent and ever-changing views of the Howgills, and you will be aware of the dramatic alteration in the landscape between the ancient Silurian and Ordovician slates of the Howgills and the longer, flatter outlines of the Carboniferous gritstones, shales and limestones of the areas to the east and south.

A particularly lovely area from Sedbergh is that around Abbot Holme and Holme Fell, best reached across the foot-bridge at Birks and the road bridge at Abbot Holme; the deep ford at Holme is impassable, however, at all but the driest times of the year, and to return to Sedbergh from a walk on Holme Fell – another splendid little viewpoint – you must continue to Middleton Bridge, cutting the corner from the caravan site by the river and then perhaps along the path beside the Rawthey by Holme Ford and the Rawthey Way back to Sedbergh. This forms an excellent half day's walk.

Further up the Lune Gorge, the Dales Way, inevitably, offers the most attractive path up from Lincoln's Inn Bridge, west of Sedbergh, to Crook of Lune. Waymarking has, of recent years, improved, and the Lune has a quite distinctive character, with some dramatic, wooded and rocky stretches. To make a circular walk back to Sedbergh either cross the river at Hole House foot-bridge, picking up the bridleway climbing up the wooded gill behind Stocks to join the lane behind Firbank Fell, or with more time available, keeping on to Crook of Lune and the old bridleway which becomes enclosed as it climbs below High House to join the Firbank road.

Whichever way you ascend Firbank, leave the road just where it becomes enclosed to climb to Fox's Pulpit, a simple crag with a plaque marking the point where, in 1652, George Fox preached his famous sermon to a thousand people, an inspired oration which was the impetus for the creation of the Society of Friends.

You can also enjoy, just over the brow of the fell, the view of the four valleys and the Howgill Fells which Sedgwick remembered so vividly.

Return to Lincoln's Inn Bridge by taking the track north of New Field Farm and the path which takes care to find – see the Sedbergh (Howgills) map – descending through the wood and across the lane at a stile to the bridge.

One of the most satisfying of all the longer walks from Sedbergh involves an ascent of Middleton Fell. Be prepared for a long and fairly strenuous day unless you can arrange to pick up one of the very infrequent weekday buses from Sedbergh to Kirkby Lonsdale for Barbon, or indeed the Dales Rail bus on a limited number of Sundays. Otherwise give yourself adequate time to cover the eight miles or so from Sedbergh to Barbon – an easy and pleasant walk via Birks, Abbot Holme, Holme Fell, the riverside bridleway, and the back lane by High Green and Millbeck.

From Barbon Church a footpath cuts across to Eskholme by the wood, and then, at Eskholme Farm climbs steeply up Eskholme Pike above Barbon Park. A steep and steady climb now, following the parish boundary, up to Castle Knott, and high above the steep side of Barbondale and on the edge of Middleton Fell up to Calf Top.

Although this is not a difficult climb – a slow steady slog is perhaps the best description – it is a stunning viewpoint; one of the best in the whole of the Dales, looking dizzily down into Barbondale, a dale which in fact follows the line of the Dent Fault, and as you follow the edge of the fell round, down into Dentdale overlooking Combe Scar, a typical mountain cwm or col. But the view over to the west is the really thrilling one, the whole coastline, if the weather is clear, virtually at your feet from Blackpool to the shipyards of Barrow. At 609 metres, or a little under 2,000 feet, Calf Top is not high, but somehow perfectly situated.

The path contours around – do not be tempted to try and descend into Dentdale; no rights of way exist and the gradient makes it dangerous in many places, with unstable screes. Follow the wall right round along Long Bank where, although the public right of way continues back westwards to Fellside, *de facto* access exists for considerate walkers over Holme Knott, descending to pick up the bridleway over Holme Fell for Sedbergh. One of the great walks of the Pennines, this is perhaps one of the least known.

Another walk for the initiated, of nothing like its epic flavour but perhaps of even more dramatic contrasts, also begins at Barbon, this time taking the bridleway alongside Barbon Beck and through the woods of Barbon Park, a quite delightful walk, to emerge in the middle of Barbondale at a fairly manageable ford over the beck; this section of the dale is a popular place for picnicking motorists in the summer months. Immediately across the road and uphill, a bridleway – difficult to see on the ground – follows Aygill to Bull Pot. From Bull Pot a well-used pot-holers' track goes towards Lancaster Hole and Ease Gill. Go some way up

Ease Gill to locate an easy point of crossing, and follow the far side of the beck down to Ease Gill Kirk, a steep and narrow limestone gorge.

You must now follow the beck downstream, through a series of stunning little gills and waterfalls, some waiting to be explored and with small caves. This is a place of great romance, atmosphere and beauty. The fact that it lies on the edges of maps does not make the beckside path easy to follow; Wainwright is the most useful guide here. The path, when it finally emerges on the Kendal and Morecambe OS map and becomes a right of way, is easy to follow descending a lovely and virtually unknown little western valley, green and wooded, quite unlike anywhere else in the Dales, indeed more like parts of the Scottish Highlands in its quietness and remoteness, until below Springs Wood it emerges at the lane from the site of Leck Mill, the village of Leck, with a beckside path to Cowan Bridge.

Cowan Bridge has a certain notoriety, being the site of the school for clergymen's daughters where the Brontë sisters suffered and which was immortalized both in Mrs Gaskell's biography of Charlotte and as Lowood in *Jane Eyre*. The original school building, though altered, still stands, with a suitable plaque and anyone seeing the present hamlet finds it difficult to imagine that it could, in the 1820s, have been such an unhealthy place. But if you read the description of Lowood in *Jane Eyre* you will see how accurately Charlotte has described the countryside, with the majestic fells you have descended in the background.

Field paths lead from Cowan Bridge to Kirkby Lonsdale or if transport is not available, the quiet lane along the line of the old Roman road or perhaps the higher fell track by Fell Yeat will get you back to Barbon.

Perhaps Kirkby Lonsdale is just a little bit too far away from the more obvious and convenient fell paths to become a real walkers' centre. This is a pity because it really is a very fine town in every way, with a number of eighteenth-century buildings of great charm and character, and a dramatic setting high above the Lune. The famous Devil's Bridge across the Lune is a splendid place to sit and stroll by, even if the parking area just by the bridge is inevitably filled with ice-cream vans, motor cycles and assorted urban comforts. Ruskin, who loved Kirkby Lonsdale and bitterly complained when the view painted by Turner from the church "one of the loveliest scenes in England" (dutifully marked by the Ordnance Survey with a viewpoint sign) was in his opinion desecrated by iron railings, tasteless benches and, worst of all, a local rubbish tip. I wonder what he would have said about the hot-dog stalls of the 1980s at Devil's Bridge.

Nonetheless, Kirkby Lonsdale, with its many welcoming cafés and pubs, and its bookshops, could not be a better place to end a walk. That, as much as anything else, makes it worth while persevering with the intricate network of little lanes and byways east of Kirkby Lonsdale to get onto the Casterton Fell tracks if only to be able, at the end of the day, to unlace one's boots at that most gracious of Dales towns.

The Howgill Fells
The high reputation the Howgill Fells have among walkers is richly deserved. They really are quite unique, a great cluster of green ridges and domes in a remarkably compact area, isolated from the rest of the Pennines by the Rawthey Valley to the east, and the Lune Gorge to the west. Unlike most of the Dales fellsides, the Howgills are almost totally unenclosed, open fellside and moorland shared by local farmers with common grazing rights, where there are Rough Fell sheep and beautiful wild fell ponies, and the occasional kestrel or buzzard. You can walk freely over them and whilst much of the walking, especially over the more popular summits (and popular is a relative term in the Howgills) is fairly easy, there are whole sections of sombre, lonely magnificence, gills of Wagnerian splendour, country of haunting beauty. And from almost everywhere on the Howgills the views, when conditions are clear, are superlative.

As always, Wainwright provides a most excellent guide for the Howgills, particularly important and useful in an area where there are few formal rights of way indicated on Ordnance maps and the Howgills are situated on the joining of no less than three 1:50,000 Ordnance sheets. Invaluable too is Arthur Gemmell's Sedbergh (Howgills) map which picks out clearly and accurately all the major tracks, routes, and major access points onto the open fell. Whilst walkers can wander freely over the fellsides, farmers are naturally extremely sensitive about anyone trying to take a short cut through lower fields and enclosures where no rights of way exist in order to get onto the fell; they are equally sensitive about cars being parked in the narrow lanes blocking entrances or restricting clearances. Gemmell assists by not only showing, with a bold red arrow, where you can get onto the fell, but places where it is usually possible to leave a car.

Sedbergh is the natural and obvious centre for the southern part of the Howgills, and a typical and highly satisfying circular walk can be enjoyed by climbing up the fell directly behind Sedbergh, keeping your height along the high ridges before descending perhaps down one of the buttresses or deep gills that penetrate into the side of the hills, and then making your way along the network of valley paths to the east or west back to Sedbergh – a combination which offers the advantage of contrast and variety.

An obvious short walk from Sedbergh onto the Howgills, and one followed by thousands of schoolboys from Sedbergh School, is to follow Joss Lane up from the car park, conveniently sign-posted "To the Fell", up beyond Hill Farm and the wooded gorge above Settlebeck Gill through the gate onto the fell, following the zigzagging track up to the cairn then directly up, a steep climb, the sharp summit dome of Winder which, as you would expect, offers a panoramic view across the whole vale and down the Lune valley, with the town stretched out below you. The best way off is to pick up the bridleway which comes in from behind and descends through the bracken to the fell wall below; follow the path parallel to the fell wall, still through bracken to the path through Lockbank Farm, keeping directly ahead along an alley-way into the town. To save returning by the main road, keep straight ahead along the school drive (a footpath) keeping beyond the school to emerge on the path behind the church.

To climb Crook, the adjacent fell to Winder, turn sharp right at the gate onto the fell crossing the beck below the waterfall and follow a green track – the Water Authority pipe track – which winds around the fell and into Ashbeck Gill, cutting off left to ascend the summit of Crook Fell to its cairn; the easiest descent is to go straight down the fell, due west back into Settlebeck Gill. For Sickers and Knott, the other two in the quartet of fells that form the back-drop to Sedbergh town, continue along the path up Ashbeck Gill past the hut and little dam at the top of the gill before swinging right up to the summit of Sickers (1,600 feet) and then along the grassy ridge to the cairn on Knott, another fine and most impressive little viewpoint; descend south-westwards to pick up the footpath around the enclosure wall, soon descending left to Castlehaw, the strange green mounds which undoubtedly were the site of a medieval motte and bailey castle, suggesting Sedbergh's importance guarding the natural pass through the valleys.

A more ambitious walk involves an ascent of The Calf, at 2,220 feet the highest summit in the Howgills. Leave Sedbergh as before along the Settlebeck Gill path, this time keeping along the side of the stream, uphill, through a narrow gorge and into a marshy hollow or col. Make your way to the top of this – the path peters out and there is little evidence of a way on the ground – to join the clear bridlepath coming up from behind Winder. Follow this up onto Arant Haw and then along a magnificent saddle of the fells – a narrow and thrilling ridge, perfectly easy and safe, but with grassy slopes descending away a thousand feet on either side of you. Keep ahead up the slope around the wire fence on the side of Calders, a fairly stiff climb to the summit (2,200 feet) then cross north-westwards over the fairly flat summit of Bram Rigg to the white trig. station on top of the Calf. Wainwright, Lakeland man though he is, has to confess, "There is not a more extensive panorama in England than this."

The most satisfying way off The Calf is to descend Cautley Spout; but great care is required to keep off the treacherous Cautley Crags. From The Calf steer north-eastwards to pick up the track to Bowderdale, then the path to the north of Cautley Holme Beck, and a steep descent under Bowderdale Head, with the spectacular Cautley Spout, a waterfall descending in stages over 700 feet, roaring through the rocky gorge beside you. The path descends to a flat-bottomed valley leading to the lovely old seventeenth-century Cross Keys Temperance Hotel (a National Trust property) at Cautley, but to return to Sedbergh cross the foot-bridge, right, before the stream reaches the main river, and pick up the bridleway which keeps above the enclosures for most of the way to Fawcett Bank, Hobdale and Thursgill before picking up the Rawthey Way at Buck Bank Farm, and the riverside path back to Sedbergh.

Cautley does, of course, provide an excellent alternative way of climbing the waterfall and up to The Calf, before returning to a car parked in the car park near the Cross Keys, by the path from

Calders and Great Dummocks down Pickering Gill. But keep away from the Crags.

Almost equally fine, however, is to leave The Calf westwards along White Fell, a long, gentle buttress descending to cross Long Rigg Beck for Castley and a choice of lane or riverside path back to Sedbergh; hardly less pleasant is the bridleway off Bram Rigg to the south curving around Bram Rigg Beck and the minor hillock of Swarth Greaves before following the enclosure wall around to Birkhaw.

But with time and energy to expend follow the grassy plateau of The Calf over Bush Howe, where immediately below the summit is the notorious "Black Horse of Busha", an outline of a horse in the dark, slaty scree, reputedly created by Iron Age man and, for some strange reason connected with primeval magic, allegedly impossible to photograph. Fell Head is another splendid viewpoint, looking across towards the Lakeland mountains; you can continue into Carling Gill via Black Force, descending to the fine old bridge at Carling Gill on the Fairmile road.

These northern parts of the Howgills remain virtually unknown – Tebay Fell, Langdale Fell and Ravenstonedale Common are difficult of access and offer few simple circular routes; an occasional Dales Rail bus skirts the northern fringe from the Kirkby Stephen–Tebay road, opening up, for example, the possibility of walking the whole length of Bowderdale from the hamlet of Bowderdale Foot before ascending The Calf by Hare Shaw and continuing over Arant Haw to Sedbergh; but unless you have two cars available this will not be a viable alternative. The best proposition, for most people, therefore, will be to consider Wainwright's suggestions of a series of starting points from Tebay to Ravenstonedale offering a series of elliptical forays – for example from Tebay up to Blease Fell, from Gaisgill to Rispa Pike, from Weasdale with its celebrated tree nurseries to Green Bell. But as these are not documented outside *Walks on the Howgill Fells* it would be wrong of me to trespass upon such admirably charted territory.

Like the valley of the Lune, the Rawthey valley provides some fascinating valley paths on both sides of the river, and convenient access points (for example at Hobdale or Fawcett Rigg) onto the open fell.

The country to the immediate east of the Rawthey is, at least superficially, less interesting; though pleasant walks can be plan-ned around the fringe of the fell, around Bluecaster and Taythes, Cross Hall and Hebblethwaite – with its ancient hall – many of the higher bridleways peter out on Baugh Fell (pronounced "bow" as in bow-tie), a most formidable and frankly dreary hill, a boggy and empty wasteland, too flat and featureless to offer the hill walker great pleasure. However, if you enjoy wild and empty landscapes, follow its southern slopes from Dowbiggin or Gars-dale foot, along the beck up to Knoutberry Haw, known by that poetic name "Ringing Keld Gutter" along the boundary wall. It is an easy walk, a test of stamina rather than strength; the views from the huge summit plateau, with its shallow tarns, are good and most certainly worth the effort of getting there, at least on a fine day. To confuse you the great end of fell overlooking Grisedale is indeed called East Baugh Fell, but the arm which extends to the north is called West Baugh Fell. Descend by Haskashaw and Grisedale Becks into Uldale. There is no way from Baugh Fell top directly into Garsdale, a valley of very few paths where even the most enthusiastic footpath hunter is forced to use the road in many places.

The route back to Sedbergh via Uldale is, on the other hand, fascinating; a right of way follows the infant Rawthey down to Uldale. Keep to the south of the beck from here, a remote and beautiful highland valley, almost totally unfrequented and ex-tremely lovely. Before Rawthey Bridge you can pick up the old road around the shoulder of Bluecaster to Bluecaster Side and a choice of footpath routes back to Sedbergh.

An alternative route off Baugh Fell is down by Grisedale Pike and into Grisedale, "The Dale that died", described as such in Barry Cockcroft's book, a remote isolated and now almost totally depopulated valley, apart from one surviving farmer and weekend cottagers. The through-path from Grisedale into Uldale or vice versa forms a shallow pass, about six miles long, through country of desolate beauty and austere grandeur, and, in Grisedale, an awesome sense of how the twentieth century has had the effect of crowding ever more of us into cities and leaving whole stretches of empty and under-productive landscape for-gotten and out of mind. For those who live in such cities, this is the other England.

The chapel in Grisedale, itself a symbol of the coherence and continuity of Dales culture, closed in 1970, the same year that trains ceased to call at Garsdale Station.

Mallerstang

Mallerstang is really the valley from the source of the Eden at Hell Gill to Kirkby Stephen, framed to the east by Mallerstang Edge and High Seat, to the west by Wild Boar Fell, intersected by the B6259 Kirkby Stephen – Hawes road and the Settle – Carlisle railway. It is a small area, outside the National Park yet by every possible criterion as fine as anything within the National Park – on a grand, heroic scale, and offering some of the finest fell walking to be had in the Pennines, including two most spectacular ridge walks.

Once again, lack of public transport restricts not only those without a car but anyone wanting to walk the full length of both major ridges; once again, Dales Rail when it runs and serves Kirkby Stephen and Garsdale stations provides the solution.

Three major routes dominate the possibilities, therefore; these can be adapted easily enough to reach a common starting and finishing-point by car.

The first of these is the ancient High Way, sometimes known as Lady Anne Clifford's Way because it was used by that formidable and energetic lady in the seventeenth century in travelling between her many castles and estates. This old green road was a major pass through the Pennines from Bronze Age times until the modern road was built through the valley in the nineteenth century. It starts from Cotter Rigg and Cotter End *en route* from Hawes, and follows the edge of High Abbotside Common round, past deserted farmhouses with the intriguing names of High Paddock, High Dyke and the High Way, crossing as it does myriad tiny streams that form the source of the River Ure, including one bearing the name of that river itself just before the track reaches Hell Gill, a deep gorge where the infant River Eden begins its long course to the Solway Firth – one of the few major rivers in England, incidentally, to flow northwards. So within a few yards on the High Way, you have crossed the watershed of England, with one beck going into the North Sea, the next making for the Irish Sea. The High Way now follows a lovely, green sward path that finally descends to join the main road through Outghill, but crossing the Eden again at Pendragon

Castle, a mysterious ruin which dates back to Norman times but, judging by its name, is even older, possibly Celtic. This was one of Lady Anne Clifford's towers and was restored by her. The way follows lanes and tracks below and around the green mound of Birkett Common, across a complex area of geological faulting with the limestones and gritstones of the Pennines suddenly giving way to the newer Permian red sandstones that dominate the Eden Valley. The highway goes by Lammerside Castle and Wharton Hall, a medieval fortified house, before joining minor lanes into Kirkby Stephen.

To ascend Mallerstang Edge, however, the walker must leave the High Way north of Hell Gill Bridge, climbing steadily to make for a point behind the crags of Hangingstone Scar and up onto Mallerstang Edge, a line of high, weathered crags high above Mallerstang. This becomes a superb high-level walk up to High Seat and High Pike with magnificent views down and along Swaledale coming into view as you ascend the crown of the ridge. Like many similar fell tops on these northern and western fringes of the Dales, choose good, clear days for them if you want to relish the splendours of long, far vistas. But in some ways best of all in Mallerstang are those bright, showery days of spring when even though for part of the time your views may be obstructed by mist and even showers, the sudden clearance of cloud perhaps swirling below you, possibly with a shaft of sunlight, can be a thrilling and quite memorable experience. Whether it is an effect of the twelve hundred feet from valley floor to peak I know not, but the valley is always resplendent with the most extraordinary effects of light and shade.

The descent from the edge is easy enough – drop down the hillside to pick up the B6270 road over Lamps Moss and follow the unfenced road down to Nateby for Kirkby Stephen – a pleasant track from Nateby leads below Hartley to the riverside footpath into Kirkby Stephen.

The third of these routes is, of course, Wild Boar Fell, a ridge walk which is simply one of the great fell walks of England. Do it from the Garsdale end, going from Garsdale Head over into Grisedale following the track by East Head and to Flust, and then climbing up onto the open fell of White Birks Common, making for the massive bulk of Swarth Fell ahead, with the cairn at its southern end. You must lose height to descend the north of

Swarth Fell swinging round to climb Wild Boar Fell and onto its flat summit.

The glory of Wild Boar Fell is the long line of crags along its eastern edge, overlooking Mallerstang, a sense of sudden, dizzy space below you, looking down into the head of Wensleydale as well as the Eden Valley, back across the Howgills, northwards to the knolls projecting ahead of the North Pennines across the Stainmoor Gap, and, most satisfying of all if conditions are fair, right across to the Solway Firth beyond the Lakeland hills to the hills of Scotland, with Crieff, in Dumfriesshire, a noticeable landmark.

There is something untamed and primitive about Wild Boar Fell, a big hill in every sense; it takes little to imagine that wild boar were hunted and the last in England shot there; millstones were fashioned from its gritstones around Sand Tarn on the summit. The entire ridge makes a perfect high-level walk.

The best descent is to continue along the same ridge down Little Fell and Greenlaw Rigg to join the lanes and tracks on Wharton Fell leading to Kirkby Stephen.

If, however, you must return to that parked car, below The Nab a bridleway crosses from Stennerskeugh to Mallerstang, emerging at a tunnel under the railway at Hazel Gill. You can either pick up the High Way from the main road about half a mile north, beginning at a field gate and ascending the fell in a remarkably straight diagonal, or take the bridleway by Hanging Lund to Aisgill, the highest point on the railway line, where, just past the waterfalls – well worth seeing – the path climbs past Hell Gill Farm to Hell Gill Bridge.

Do not follow the more obvious track from Hell Gill which descends to Shaw Paddock; bear left uphill to keep your height above the fine ruined farm of High Hall.

A number of connecting paths descend from the High Way to Garsdale and the welcoming Moorcock Inn. The best is not a right of way throughout, but cuts past the former youth hostel at Shaws (look for a stile in the wall above) past the strange and rather beautiful little lodge, adjacent to a narrow little gill with some superb little waterfalls. Below Shaws is Lunds Church, one of the tiniest churches in the Dales, a building of austere and moving simplicity surrounded by a few simple tombstones in an open grass-covered graveyard. But we are now in Upper Wensleydale.

Ascents can, of course, be made of Wild Boar Fell from Aisgill in Mallerstang or from Stennerskeugh or even Uldale to the west. None of these has the advantage of utilizing the great ridge of which Wild Boar in particular forms a part, and for my money ridge walking is the most exciting and satisfying fell walking of all. The ascent from the west is, moreover, incredibly dull, an unrelieved hard slog whose only saving grace comes from the final moments as the full open spaces below the summit come into view – a sense of surprise and drama that compensates for the slow slog uphill.

It should not be imagined however, that this is purely an area for hardened fell walkers. A very delightful and certainly not a strenuous day could be had from Garsdale Head, for example, reached by car or by rail, wandering over into Grisedale, perhaps taking the bridleway over Turner Hill to Aisgill, enjoying the waterfall at Hell Gill and its little ravine, before tracing the old High Way, perhaps as far as High Dyke to enjoy the splendid views down Wensleydale, and through the fields by Blades to the Moorcock. Or, at the far side of Mallerstang, to begin from Kirkby Stephen, a pleasant little town very well equipped with cafés and shops to cater for the needs of visitors, a very delightful short day's walk might be devised going along the riverside to join the old track to Nateby, crossing the river behind the village to Wharton Hall and Lammerside and on to Pendragon, perhaps returning along the far side of the river along the network of paths by Ridding House and Kitchen Gill back into Nateby.

But to end this section on another more heroic note, just above Kirkby Stephen, forming a marvellous outer beacon of the Yorkshire Dales, lies Nine Standards Rigg. The easiest way is to follow the riverside path reached from the foot-bridge just beyond the Buttermarket car park, along the river and straight ahead to join the track which climbs up above Hartley Quarry; there is also a more circuitous route following the right of way along Rigg Beck by Ladthwaite. Both routes will take you up Hartley Fell, an area close to the Pennine Fault and with a surprising number of limestone outcrops – a veritable little Malham – on the slopes overlooking the Stainmoor Gap. The bridleway ascends Faraday Gill then swings round the side of the fell to make for the summit, Nine Standards.

The Nine Standards are a series of quite astonishing dry-stone

River Dee by Stone House, Cowgill, Dent

Deepdale, evening

The summit of Wild Boar Fell

On Mallerstang Edge

Muker, Swaledale, from the Pennine Way

Along the Corpse Way, Kisdon, Swaledale

Near West Burton, Wensleydale

Upper Wensleydale

Lunds Church, Upper Wensleydale

Dales Rail train at Garsdale Station

Brimham Rocks, Nidderdale

How Stean Gorge, Upper Nidderdale

Arthur Adamson Memorial Bridge, Washburndale

Pen y Ghent – on the Pennine Way

Wild Boar Fell, from the High Way

Ribblehead Viaduct

pillars or cairns, crudely but strongly built out of the scattered flags and stones. There are now far more than nine of them, and their origin is quite uncertain. According to romantic legend they were constructed at the time of the raids of marauding Scots in the somewhat fond hope that the raiders would see the nine "standards" and imagine them to be the standard-bearers of a mighty army. More likely they are some kind of ancient boundary or territorial marking, a method of solving disputes; they make a mighty landmark and a glorious viewpoint. They also stand on the edge of some bleak and inhospitable countryside, notwithstanding, in recent years, the comforting presence of the Coast to Coast path to them. Return along the same bridleway you came along, but where this bends back towards Faraday Gill, keep ahead and left to join the main road over Lamps Moss and walk along its grassy verge to Nateby from where there is a choice of routes back into Kirkby Stephen.

REFERENCE

Maps
Ordnance Surrey Landranger 1:50,000 Sheet 91 Appleby; 97 Kendal and Morecambe; 98 Wensleydale and Wharfedale
The Sedbergh Footpath Map, Arthur Gemmell (Yorkshire Dales National Park)
The Sedbergh (Howgills) Footpath Map, Arthur Gemmell (Stile Maps)

Books
Walks in Limestone Country, W. A. Wainwright (Westmorland Gazette, 1970)
Walks on the Howgill Fells, W. A. Wainwright (Westmorland Gazette, 1972)
Walking in the Craven Dales, Colin Speakman (Dalesman, 1973)
The Dale that Died, Barry Cockcroft (Dent, 1978)

9

Swaledale

It is hardly surprising that for many ramblers, Swaledale is their favourite Yorkshire Dale. Its remoteness and its feeling of a perfect harmony between man and nature, give an illusion at least of a rural paradise which refugees from urban civilization can, for a short time at least, share.

The fact that it was once a busy industrial valley, with the string of villages along the main road serving hillsides pocked with mine shafts, water-wheels, crushing mills and washing floors, bringing out lead ore in vast quantities, must qualify this idyllic view of old Swaledale. Another interesting feature is the incredible ferocity of the River Swale itself, a true mountain river whose destructive force undercutting banks and walls makes it easily the fiercest river in Yorkshire.

Not that anyone would wish to deny "Swa'dle's" astonishing, romantic beauty, the visual splendours particularly in the higher reaches of the dale which, in recent years, through the novels and television films of James Herriot have given the area, with Wensleydale, the name "Herriot Country". Such epithets are excellent for the tourist trade, and tourism that brings in wealth to assist a sadly declining population, can only be welcomed. "James Herriot" would, no doubt, be the very first to agree that the spectacular nature of the countryside and the character of the local community have given his books much of their appeal; he has only told the truth, and the fame of the Yorkshire vet can only enhance the probability that future generations will seek to keep the unspoiled beauty of Swaledale as it is. The empty moorlands with their derelict workings are a vivid reminder of the decline and collapse not only of a great industry, but the way of life it sustained. Ironically, conservationists would now arise in bitter opposition were the old Swaledale mines to be reopened, concerned, very properly, with the pollution the mines would cause. Only farming and tourism remain to keep the residual communities ticking over; Swaledale has a declining and ageing population. Perhaps a combination of tourism and appropriate kinds of small-scale light industries can provide the solution in areas like the northern Dales to return the villages to life. Behind the haunting beauty of Swaledale there is a melancholia, a sense of the many Dalesmen, the same whose boots carved out the hilltracks or village paths, who generations ago left for the new factories of Tyneside or Lancashire, or who emigrated across "'t girt dub" – the Atlantic – to take their skills and creative energies to the United States.

The hill walker will never be far from the signs of past industry in Swaledale, evident even in the little farmsteads and smallholdings kept by men who were both miners and farmers, and whose little allotments of land provided welcome additional income. Most of their cottages are at best, in the 1980s, weekend cottages. At worst their roofs gape to the weather.

But as walking country Swaledale can only be described as superb. It has great contrasts in a very small area, much to delight the naturalist, the archaeologist, and the historian. For convenience I divide the dale into three main sections, mid-Swaledale based on Richmond, the upper valley based on Reeth, and Arkengarthdale, the major tributary valley and a dale rich in interest.

One sad deficiency at the present time in Swaledale is the absence of good walkers' maps. Even the 1:50,000 map, barely adequate for detailed exploration of the Swaledale footpath network, leaves poor Swaledale hacked about the edge of three sheets – 98, 99 and 92. There are at present no Second Series 1:25,000 sheets and the First Series are virtually useless for the walker in that they do not show rights of way. Fortunately there are plans for an Outdoor Leisure Series for the northern Dales and Stile Maps plan a Swaledale Map. Swaledale will not forever be uncharted territory.

Mid-Swaledale
Richmond is the kind of town which is so impressive with its Norman castle perched on a rock high above the Swale, and its cluster of houses and cottages around it, that you marvel that it is

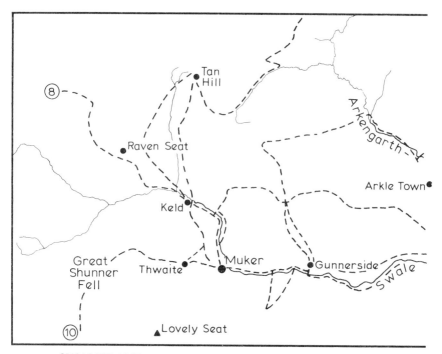

SWALEDALE

not somehow more renowned, more famous. Doubtless it would be if it were in the south of England rather than in a remoter part of North Yorkshire. In truth, it is far more than a place to start a walk from. It demands time to be spent in it, to loiter around its quiet courts and "wynds", to savour its marvellous mixture of the medieval and eighteenth century. And it is still a garrison town, with the huge army camp at Catterick only just over the hill, and soldiers, everywhere in evidence.

Its railway line was an early victim of the Beeching axe leaving its historic station under a preservation order that unfortunately did not extend to the railway lines and the trains. There is, however, a reasonably convenient bus service from Darlington, a town served by Inter-City and 125 high-speed trains from many parts of England along the East Coast Main Line, making day trips with one or more of British Rail's bargain fares a distinct possibility. United Buses operate via Richmond to Wensleydale and Swaledale and, in the summer months, special Explorer tickets will allow you to travel to the head of both Dales.

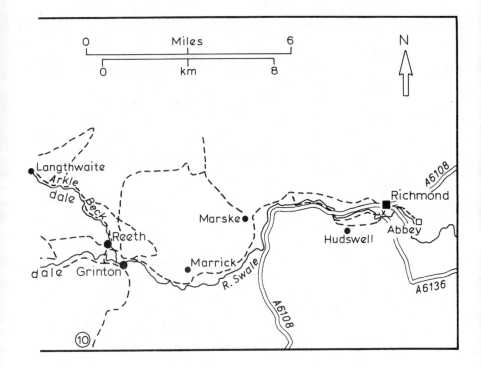

There are a number of pleasant short walks from Richmond which can be combined with time spent exploring the town, the castle, and the eighteenth-century theatre. From the riverside path below the castle, you can follow the riverside along the tarmac path to Eastby Abbey, founded in 1155 by the Constable of Richmond Castle for an order of Premonstratensian canons. It is generally considered to be one of the most picturesque of all the many monastic ruins in North Yorkshire.

Upstream from Richmond Bridge is a magnificent woodland walk, following the narrow gorge of the Swale, through National Trust woodlands as far as Hag Wood. You can take the path up to the village of Hudswell, perhaps following the path through the little wooded gorge that emerges alongside Hudswell Church, walking along the lane through the village and either returning to Richmond along the path from Hudswell that follows the top of the wood above the Swale, or keeping along the lane towards Holly Hill before cutting across down to Richmond by a path that gives superb views of the town and castle. A certain young man named Joseph Mallord William Turner seemed to think so too and the water-colour he produced is one of the most famous of his picturesque views of the north of England. For that reason alone it is worth climbing up through the woods to Hudswell.

Another very fine panoramic walk from Richmond is to Applegarth and Willance's Leap. Take the lane which leaves the A6108 on the right soon after the Marske road – marked as a white lane on the OS map. Where the tarmac ends a track goes on to Whitcliffe Wood and below Whitcliffe Scar; you can either continue along the path beyond Applegarth to Clapgate, or go up to the main Marske road before picking up the path along the top of Whitcliffe Scar, past the monument erected to commemorate Robert Willance's extraordinary leap of 1606 which Robert Willance, if not his horse, survived. The path rejoins the farm road to Richmond.

Oddly enough part of this walk is included in one of the first ramblers' guidebooks ever written, *Excursions in Yorkshire by the North Eastern Railway* by John Phillips in 1853. Geoffrey White's *Walks in Swaledale* of 1980 provides a more up-to-date version.

The area immediately to the south and south-east of Richmond is dominated by the military, both in the form of Catterick Garrison and Ministry of Defence lands, tank ranges and shooting areas, closed to the public and marked on the map as Danger Areas. Warning notices exist around the perimeter of such areas to deter any would-be ramblers. The Yorkshire Dales are perhaps fortunate in being extensive enough to absorb military activity and training in fairly significant areas, outside National Park boundaries, which are in no sense critical amenity areas, unlike the equivalent areas of Dartmoor and the Dorset coast. But ramblers must leave such areas well alone.

Marske and Marrick have, however, plenty to offer. You can, of course, follow the Applegarth tracks beyond Clapgate along a footpath to Marske, and then along an attractive combination of quiet lane and footpath past Marrick Priory and on to Grinton and Reeth. If you consult the United timetables a tea-time bus is available most days (not Sundays outside the summer months) to take you back into Richmond.

Very pleasant circular walks can be planned from both Marske and Marrick. A way of taking one such walk is to leave a car in Marske – an untypical Dales village of rather grand houses – and to follow Marske Beck via Orgate and Telfit to Helwith, returning down the track along the other side of the valley. Take care not to wander too far north along the tributary of Marske Beck, however, up Throstle Gill, beyond the Marske – Newsham road, onto Gayle Moor which is also an army practising range.

A circular walk offering fine views of the Dales can be planned between Marrick and Marske via Nun Cotes, Ellers and Hollins Farm, returning by the bridleway along the valley side via Low Oxque and Marrick Park. A dominant feature on this walk is the obelisk to Matthew Hutton, 1814, high on the hillside above Hollins Farm.

Marrick, of course, is celebrated for its priory, a Benedictine Foundation of the twelfth century, the ruins of which have been converted into a youth residential centre. One of the most fascinating stretches of footpath in the Dales connects the priory with the village, the so-called Nun's Causey, a stone staircase through the woods. A very dramatic circular walk perhaps to and from Reeth can be completed by following the riverside track from Reeth and Fremington past Marrick Priory, up the Nun's Causey to Marrick and back up the lane from Marrick along Fremington Edge, a high-level path following the curve of the fell round into Arkengarthdale before reaching the track back down into High Fremington and Reeth.

Upper Swaledale

Reeth offers a fine choice of walks and indeed, with its good facilities including an excellent folk museum with many lead-mining remains, is probably the most convenient centre if you want to spend two or three days in Upper Swaledale. A whole spider's web of footpaths radiates around the village, along the valley bottom or up onto the moorland north or south. An attractive walk can be enjoyed following the lane along the south of the village which becomes a track, and then a path to Healaugh; if you turn left at the first junction, the path leads to the little suspension bridge over the Swale, and to an ancient bridleway, crossing a prehistoric earthwork – probably Celtic – before emerging below Swale Hall at Grinton Church, the ancient parish church of Swaledale. From the Grinton Bridge a field path crosses to the Arkle Beck and follows the beckside by Old Fremington Mill and the road to Reeth – though footpath users will look out for the path that doubles back on the left-hand side under the road bridge to emerge in the back of the village.

This walk is described in great detail in a pamphlet produced by the National Park Department and written by Lawrence Barker, the Swaledale Area Warden and local expert on lead mining. It is on sale at National Park Centres and many local shops. Another of Lawrence's pamphlets follows the track by Reeth School to a moorland path by The Riddings, before descending to Healaugh, and then picking up the riverside path back to Reeth.

South of the river, attractive paths radiate onto Harkerside Moor; not all are distinct and some need care to find. It is also an area rich in ancient remains, Maiden Castle a mysterious, perhaps Bronze Age ring, and evidence of various kinds of workings from the lead-mining days.

A fine walk is to trace a route up Harkerside Moor, perhaps along Grinton Gill, before hitting the road to Redmire, and cutting back across the moorland along the path signed to Castle Bolton to the summit of Greets Hill. This continues along the track down and out of Apedale another valley rich in lead-mining remains; those with an interest in industrial archaeology might well complete the circuit from Apedale by cutting back across to the main road and continuing back along Cobscar, before turning back northwards over the path over Redmire Moor and Grinton Moor with its massive flue and smelt mill. From Grinton Lodge, the castellated youth hostel, a delightful path leads down Cogden Gill to the main road just east of Grinton.

But it is very satisfying to continue from Apedale back up the hillside and East Bolton Moor to Castle Bolton, if for no other reason than to end a walk at such a lovely village and romantic ruin. Bus users will find no problem in getting back – both the Swaledale and Wensleydale services operate to and from Richmond with a connection to Darlington.

Gunnerside Gill is another paradise for industrial archaeologists. Parking is limited in the village, so if you are exploring the gill, leave your car where it will not be a nuisance. A good, well-waymarked path goes up the gill from the bridge over Gunnerside Beck, and the gill itself, steep, narrow and lonely, is an awesome sight, with hushes (deep grooves in the hillside artificially created using the scouring action of water to expose the lead ores), levels, remains of water-wheel pits, spoil heaps, water channels, and, at the head of the curious Y-shaped valley, the remains of Blakethwaite smelt mill and great peat store. It is all oddly moving, relics of a great industry, now merely a ghost. A number of specialist guides are in existence on the lead mines of Swaledale and the techniques used, perhaps most vividly captured by the late Thomas Armstrong, who lived for many years in Swaledale, in his powerful novel *Adam Brunskill*.

There are interesting possibilities once you are at the top of Gunnerside Gill – to pick up the shooting track at the far side of the gill, to pick up moorland paths eastwards over the moor to Hard Level Gill, or westwards into Swinnergill, making your way through moorlands scarred with old workings, back into the main valley through a wide choice of miners' tracks and ways.

If you are returning to Gunnerside village, perhaps the pleasantest way is to climb up the hillside on the same side as the path you followed from Gunnerside, about the mid-point of the gill above the remains of the Sir Francis Mine, climbing up above the lip of the gill with quite breathtaking views down the narrow gorge and following the path past those little miners' smallholdings around Winterings, descending into Gunnerside as it were from above.

This is an area rich in history and archaeology, with an old, complex pattern of settlement dating perhaps from those original Danish and Viking settlers (the name Gunnerside is derived from Gunner's Saetre, Old Norse for Gunner's dwelling) who first cleared those isolated ravines and hollows.

High above Gunnerside Gill is Rogan's Seat, an easy walk over the open moorland. But this is shooting country and no formal access exists. Proceed in a spirit of courtesy.

Swaledale is, as I hope this chapter implies, a complex area; it has many paths, many possibilities, many deep secluded gills. An author who names them all keeps no secrets. The maps exist for you to discover them for yourself.

But one or two are well enough documented elsewhere to permit others to share. Ivelet Bridge, easily reached from Gunnerside by means of the path from Gunnerside Bridge or by field path from Gunnerside, is a famous single-arch bridge on the old corpse road from the higher settlements to Grinton, once the only church with hallowed grounds to bury the dead. Just across the road from Ivelet Bridge a path crosses a stile to climb up the side of

Oxnop Gill, one of those magical ravines with sparkling falls that Swaledale excels in. Follow the path up, away from the beck and along the top of the wooded ravine before it crosses rough pasture to the Oxnop Scar road. A path branches off, left, back over the gill to High Oxnop, cutting across to the mine track by Gill Head, and back to the main road at Satron for Gunnerside. Or, adventurous, you might persevere along the quiet road to pick up one of the moorland tracks leading down into Wensleydale, to Askrigg or even Carperby.

Muker is perhaps the most photographed village in Swaledale. The setting is perfect, the scatter and huddle of cottages and barns around the little village church arranged as it were for the camera. From Muker, paths lead into the area around Kisdon, one of the most marvellous little areas to explore on foot in the Yorkshire Dales. You can, of course, simply follow the Pennine Way up to Keld, up along the shoulder of the hill high above the Swale – the views from this path are unforgettable, and it is little wonder that Tom Stephenson considers this perhaps the loveliest single piece of the Pennine Way. Or you can follow the path along the valley bottom, equally lovely in its way, to Keld; or cross the river at the foot-bridge about half a mile north of the village which takes you onto the riverside path back to Muker or north to Keld; or you can climb the old corpse way, high over Kisdon Hill, itself a geological freak from the Ice Age when the waters of Swale were diverted to the east of the hill to carve out a new valley.

Such a choice of ways makes it possible to work out a number of delightful walks simply between Keld and Muker; add to this the hamlet of Thwaite, just to the west, birthplace of the famous Kearton brothers the naturalists, photographers and broadcasters, and now the site of the Kearton Guest-House and Restaurant known and beloved by ramblers throughout the north of England, and you begin to comprehend why so many people return time and again to Swaledale. The waterfalls near Keld are justly famous. They include Kisdon Force on the main river just below Keld, East Gill or Catrake Force on the beck of that name that joins the Swale at Keld, and Wain Wath (meaning literally ford for carts) about a mile north of the hamlet.

This is a place for the walker, not the motorist. There is very little room to leave a car, and certainly not a coach in Muker, Thwaite or Keld. Keld is an extraordinary little hamlet, a place which feels like the world's end, which in a sense it is, tucked away on the apex of a triangle of roads down by the river and surrounded by countryside of exquisite beauty.

But even Keld is full of the ghosts of the old miners. Follow the track, for example, that leaves the Pennine Way behind East Gill and climbs up the fellside by the superbly named Crackpot Hall, now, alas, a ruin. Its name derives not from the mental state of the last inhabitants but "pot" (i.e. pot-hole or cave) of the crows. Behind Crackpot Hall a path climbs up into Swinner Gill, another awesome Swaledale ravine, not as long or as steep as Gunnerside Gill, but in its way even more impressive, with the all-too-evident relics of the lead industry scattered in the valley and in the quiet hillside.

For those with a little patience and care, find your way right up to the head of the gill where, behind a waterfall, there is a secret cave. Unless you go after prolonged dry weather expect to get wet before you get in. Once inside you can almost stand, the roof is carved like the crude silhouette of a man. This is Swinner Gill Kirk, allegedly where persecuted Catholics met and prayed in the darkest days of their suffering. It seems a strange tale – having struggled so far to such a remote place there would be little need to pray in a cave. But it adds romance to a place which needs little more romance.

If you have found your way to Swinner Gill Kirk, you will not have too much trouble returning down the far side of the valley down the track to Muker.

Beyond Keld true wilderness begins. A few walkers stray into Birkdale or Whitsun Dale, West Stones Dale or onto Ravenseat. It is an empty, bleak landscape. The Pennine Way and Coast to Coast Walk cross the area on vertical and horizontal axes; beyond these well-used routes the land belongs to the ubiquitous Swaledale sheep and the curlews.

Arkengarthdale

The road from Reeth to Tan Hill with its branch over Stang Forest to Barnard Castle and Teesdale serves a remote and scattered community and hamlets of great character – Langthwaite, Arkle Town, Whaw. The presence of the remains of the great lead-mining industry is almost oppressive – great earthworks, remains of huge activity, the skeletal shapes or forms of buildings.

Not many walkers know Arkengarthdale. Perhaps more obvious and self-evident beauties are too close, or perhaps when motoring through, the bleakness of the surrounding moors suggests little of interest in the hollows or by the becks. Nothing could be further from the truth. There is, in Arkengarthdale, great charm, a delicacy, even intimacy of scale. Take, for a pleasant surprise, if you do not yet know it, the riverside path from Reeth right up the Arkle Beck to Whaw, starting from the far side of Reeth Bridge below Fremington Edge and meandering to and from the river. The footpath is, I believe, marginally better than the nearby bridleway, a quiet, secluded and utterly charming little way, rich with the remnants of former activity, old workings, mine tailings, now totally grassed over and blending into the greenness of the landscape.

Cross the little foot-bridge into Arkle Town; a very pleasant circular walk back to Reeth can be made along the field path at the other side of the river that eventually emerges at the main road just above Reeth. But it is worth continuing on to Langthwaite, the "capital" of Arkengarthdale, and a hamlet somehow marvellously self-contained, with its little inn and its church, above, on the roadside. You can follow the dale up through Scar House Wood and behind the ornate, almost Scottish baronial mid-Victorian Scar House, an unusual style for the Dales, now a private hotel, to the Stang Road. Alternatively, from the church, go along the track behind the distinctive white C.B. Inn (the initials C.B. stand for Charles Bathurst, local landowner and mining entrepreneur). Continue along the riverside footpath north of Arkle Beck to Whaw, that most isolated little settlement. From Whaw, tracks and paths radiate and if you are returning to Reeth (the only public transport, in fact, is the school bus operated by Harker's as far as Langthwaite), tracks and paths along either the edge of the moor, or higher up among the mine workings, lead back into the main valley of the Swale, perhaps over the side of Calver, that most distinctive of Swaledale hills.

A most attractive little circular walk (described in Geoffrey White's useful little guide) is to go from Langthwaite via Storthwaite Hall up Slei Gill with its waterfalls, returning back along the Moresdale road to Scar Top and Langthwaite Scar. One of the classic lead-mine walks is to go up from Surrender Mill on the Feetham–Langthwaite road, climbing up past Old Gang Mill perhaps going over by Hard Level Gill to Gunnerside Gill or over into Punchard Gill, with a choice of moorland tracks back to your starting-point. Punchard Gill is, indeed, very fine, with a long twisting track climbing right over the moor, in theory, at least, to Tan Hill. But the going is very rough indeed at the Tan Hill end, and the track virtually indistinguishable. Very much pleasanter is to turn north-eastwards up William Gill, a steep and beautiful ravine, back to the main road, maybe reaching Tan Hill, if you loathe road walking, by means of the unmetalled track going north towards Bowes to join the Pennine Way northwards or south-westwards up Frumming Beck to Tan Hill and West-stonedale down to Keld and Swaledale.

This is bleak, totally inhospitable country, best avoided in mist or low cloud, but glorious in clear weather. Wherever you turn there are signs of industry – tracks, hushes, old mills, evidence of human activity. It is a landscape which you either like or you do not. For me, it is reminiscent of Cornwall, not the Cornwall of the spectacular coast and beaches, but the high moors and the tin mines. Of course it is a quite different landscape, yet that epic quality remains; not a mountain landscape as on those high, spectacular western fells where the epic is that of nature; but a human epic, the struggle of generations of men to win a living underneath the bleak soil. They have left signs of that epic struggle on the landscape and wherever you turn its sombre poetry is there for the reading.

REFERENCE

Maps
Ordnance Survey Landranger 1:50,000 Sheet 91 Appleby; 92 Barnard Castle and Richmond; 98 Wensleydale and Wharfedale; 99 Northallerton and Ripon

Books
Walking in the Northern Dales, Ramblers' Association (Dalesman, 1973)
Walking in Swaledale, Geoffrey White (Dalesman, 1976, 1980)
A History of Swaledale, Edmund Cooper (Dalesman, 1969)
The Lead Industry of Wensleydale and Swaledale
Vol I The Mines
Vol II The Smelting Mills, Arthur Raistrick (Moorland, 1975)

10

Wensleydale

Wensleydale, so broad and so pastoral, is grossly underrated by walkers. There is often an underlying assumption that the dale is somehow rather dull, rather bland compared with the heady delights of Wharfedale or Swaledale.

There is, indeed, less to make you catch your breath with the sheer magical beauty of mountain or ravine. Its breadth allows you to believe as you travel down one of its main roads by car or coach that you have seen it all, that those broad green fields and flat-topped fells with their characteristic stepped edges, are, after all, a little too predictable, a shade too dull to offer the serious walker the dramatic contrasts and the sheer exuberance of fell edge and ravine for which his essentially romantic nature craves.

Nothing could be further from the truth. Wensleydale at least as much, and probably rather more than any other dale, only unfolds its real treasures for the walker. It is a subtle, small-scale beauty, with less of the total grandeur of the dales to the west, but many surprises, areas of quite exhilarating loveliness which viewed from the motor road seem merely prosaic. Like Swaledale, and, to a degree Dentdale, it shares that isolation from the major centres of population that gives it a special sense of identity, a sense of introspection and independence; not surprisingly Wensleydale has, in the past and in the present, some of the most individualistic of Dales characters. That individuality is somehow in the landscape, in the unexpected twist and turn of a gill, the juxtaposition of wood and stream, the angle of a fell, the simple yet vigorous beauty of the villages, unspoiled even into the late twentieth century.

Another surprising feature is that it takes its name not from its river, the Ure, but from a relatively modest village, Wensley, part way up the valley. Logically, the old name "Yoredale", used by

geologist John Phillips to describe the famous series of limestones, should have stuck. The name is still sometimes used for
the section of valley below Leyburn. But how Wensley came to
give its name to the main valley is, for me, a mystery unsolved,
and, I suspect, part of that very individuality and even perversity
which is part of Wensleydale's charm.

For convenience I divide Wensleydale into three sections –
Lower Wensleydale, south of Ripon and including the tributary
valley Colsterdale and its surrounding moors; Mid-Wensleydale
to include Coverdale, Bishopdale and the area between Leyburn
and Askrigg, and Upper Wensleydale west of Bainbridge and the
tributary valleys, including the valley of the River Bain and
Raydaleside.

Lower Wensleydale
There is some remarkably fine countryside around the cathedral
city of Ripon, a natural boundary of the Yorkshire Dales, where
the eastern foothills of the Pennines finally flatten out into the
plain of York. The local Ramblers' Association's excellent little
guidebook, *Walks Around Ripon* provides numerous suggestions
for anyone wishing to explore the area in detail, though it is only
fair to warn that path finding in the area needs care as the local
authority's interpretation of its footpath maintenance responsibilities in these lean times appears to be to do the absolute legal
minimum – and sometimes not even that. The compensation is to
be able to walk quiet and little-frequented paths, through countryside well-wooded with copses and pheasant shoots, a fair
proportion of arable fields (ploughed out paths are as common a
problem in Lower Wensleydale as in lowland Britain) with often
magnificent views from these same low foothills eastwards across
the flat lands, to the huge, brooding bulk of the North York
Moors.

A classic walk, deservedly in every guidebook, is from Ripon or
its outskirts to Studley Park and Fountains Abbey. I prefer to walk
there from the centre of the town, easily reached by regular buses
from Harrogate and Leeds. Take the footpath from the main
Leeds road at the little park by the Skell and follow a strange little
valley with evidence of a forgotten canal project – an abortive
extension of the historic Ripon Canal, continue along lanes and
tracks to Whitcliffe and Mackershaw, before going through the

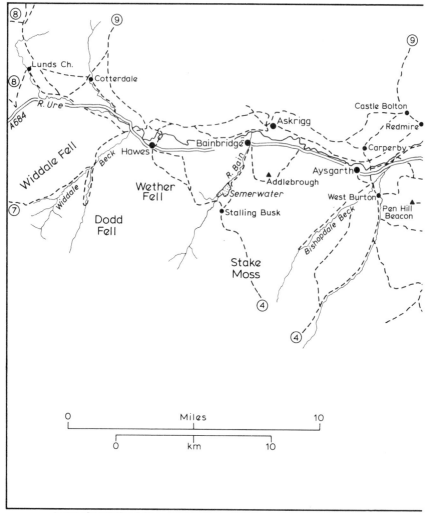

WENSLEYDALE

lovely "valley of the Seven Bridges" a series of artificial bridges over the Skell and the lake at the eastern entrance of the Fountains Abbey estate. There is, of course, no right of way through the Studley Royal Gardens and the entrance fee to the abbey is not cheap even by the standards of the 1980s; but your donation provides funds for the upkeep of this superb, publicly owned estate so do not regret the sacrifice.

These grounds, exquisitely landscaped as they are, are a visual delight: hedges, lakes, and, high up on the top path to the left

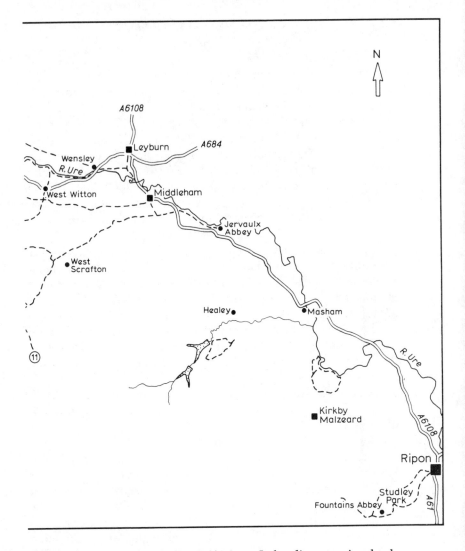

(look for the track near the Half-Moon Lake disappearing back through an artificial tunnel uphill), go by splendid temples and an eighteenth-century summer-house. The abbey itself is immensely beautiful, undoubtedly the most splendid and extensive Cistercian ruin in England, offering much for the historian to savour, as insight into the organization and wealth that created these buildings and the changing circumstances that led to its downfall. Its link with the great sheep walks of the higher Dales and the medieval port of York and, beyond the North Sea and the

Channel, the Renaissance city states of Venice and Florence is an amazing one, and remains a moving reminder of how important the wool trade of Yorkshire was to our nation's emergence as a major maritime and trading power.

Go to Fountains in late February or early March, when the banks of wild snowdrops are breathtaking in their beauty.

There is no better way back to Ripon than via the splendid eighteenth-century parkland of Studley Royal, again like the gardens, a testimony to the vision and taste of John Aislabie, the failed Chancellor of the Exchequer at the time of the South Sea Bubble financial scandal early in the eighteenth century who retired to Studley to landscape his estates.

Leave by the western entrance and, sparing the time to visit the magnificent Fountains Hall, a rare early Renaissance Jacobean house built from stone pillaged from the abbey, climb up the lane to the right, before taking the track, right, uphill, to the great obelisk at the far end of the deer park. The right of way crosses the Studley Royal parkland – you will almost certainly see one of the herds of roe-deer leaping across the skyline at some point – with the outline of Ripon Cathedral on a direct bearing between the church, the obelisk and entrance gates; this was no accident. If you look at your map carefully you will see the right of way enters Studley Roger village to the north of the busy main gateway – directly across the road at Studley Roger a ginnel leads to an obvious field path back to Ripon.

You can, of course, follow the footpath right up the Skell from Fountains into Spa Gill Wood for Grantley, returning by one or more field paths via Sawley; this is a very attractive circular walk and can be combined with a visit to the abbey.

Further north a whole network of paths and ancient ways converge on Kirkby Malzeard, a village which once had some importance as a market town. But it is all intensively farmed land, little walked and requiring great care. Until Second Series 1:25,000 maps are available for the area, it is advisable to have First Series 1:25,000 upon which you have taken the trouble to transfer the rights of way from the smaller scale sheet. Otherwise path finding, from experience, whilst always enjoyable, can have more than its reasonable quota of frustrations.

Grewelthorpe is another larger village with an interesting history, but nothing in the neighbourhood is more fascinating than Hack Fall Woods, an example of the phenomenon of a popular tourist attraction which has unaccountably been forgotten. Hack Fall Woods once attracted men of taste and discernment from throughout Britain, featuring in all the picturesque guides such, for example, as Thomas Pennant's tour from Alston Moor to Harrogate in the 1770s. You can still get there. Turn right on the road from Grewelthorpe to Masham at Oak Bank, to follow the right of way to the riverside and go down river through a wooded ravine, with the river roaring through below you; an immensely impressive sight. A ruined temple, a cave where once lived a hermit and the remains of a carriage track are silent witnesses to those be-periwigged lovers of the Gothic who came to soak up their impressions of the sublime. Expect some rather interesting path finding before you make your way on the field path back to Grewelthorpe (fainthearts should make for the Mickley road), but Hack Fall really is an extraordinary experience.

Slightly better known is the Druid's Temple, a Gothic folly up on the wooded hillside above Ilton. You can reach it easily enough from either Healey or Ilton (west of Masham), or by taking a car up to the picnic place at the end of Knowle Lane beyond High Knowle Farm. Geoffrey White suggests a pleasant circular walk in his useful *Walks in Wensleydale* to take in the "temple" and nearby forest and farm tracks. The "temple" is in fact a delightful example of how a landowner with a taste for a decaying ruin, if he was not lucky enough to possess one, would have one built, in a state of strictly tasteful decay, to add the right tone of melancholia to his romantic landscape.

This valley from Masham up to the high moors, followed by the River Burn, with its branch to the Leighton Reservoirs, is Colsterdale, one of the quietest and least visited of all Yorkshire Dales, probably only glimpsed by the occasional motorist climbing out of Nidderdale over the top to Masham. It is fine, open country, offering extensive views, and again, walkers could do worse than utilizing Geoffrey White's suggestion to make a high-level circular walk from Gollinglith to High Agra and along the moortop to the summit of Witton Fell.

Jervaulx Abbey, further north on the Ure, offers many very attractive possibilities. My own favourite is to start from Middleham, a most attractive old Dales town with Richard III's imposing castle, taking the field path over William's Hill, an earlier motte and bailey mound, to the River Cover and a riverside path down stream to Cover Bridge and its inn, then the lovely riverside path to Jervaulx Abbey and its park.

If February is the time to go to Fountains, visit Jervaulx in April when the ancient walls blaze purple with aubretias, hanging like purple carpets over and between the grey mossy stones. If you must get back to that parked car, make a circuit up by Ellingstring and Moor Cote to the village of East Witton – a perfect Anglian "defence village" around its green – by Cover Bridge and perhaps the little walled lane (very attractive) back to Middleham.

Mid-Wensleydale

Middleham is a centre for some interesting walks; a number of old tracks and ways (marked as black lines on the map) are in fact ancient roads, offering additional possibilities onto the Low Moor and High Moor, and, into Coverdale, onto Braithwaite Moor and Calbergh Moor. An attractive way to Calbergh is following path or bridleway over the Cover to Braithwaite Farm, following the path along the side of the hill below Castle Steads to Castlebergh, making your way up dale perhaps via West Scrafton to Carlton, then over the shoulder of Pen Hill to West Witton, and perhaps back to Wensley along the riverside or through Bolton Park, and the field path along the south side of the river to Middleham Bridge. There are many possible variations on this theme.

Coverdale is another of those quiet valleys that has yet to attract its fair share of ramblers. Again, it has, like Swaledale, the "split in the map" problem, and many obvious and attractive walks are simply not evident until you place two maps together, with an awkward map seam to negotiate.

The riverside path along the dale can be followed as far as Woodale, but it is probably more sensible to follow the old road up from Arkleside – having first of all, no doubt, branched off to Horsehouse with its excellent little inn – climbing up the gill to pick up the bridleway back over Swineside Moor to West Scrafton. This is a very attractive walk, combining a mountain riverside in one direction, with high-level walking in the reverse direction.

There are several moorland tracks and ways out of Coverdale to the adjacent dales which, if you have solved the perhaps horrendous problems of transport or do not mind a fairly heavy day's walk to make a circular trip possible, offer exciting possibilities. From West Scrafton there are ways right over the top into Nidderdale, as indeed there is from Arkle over the ominously named Dead Man's Hill, the latter joining another ancient pack-horse track over Little Whernside and into Wharfedale. In the other direction tracks cross Carlton Moor into Walden, with the paths up to Fleensop offering interesting possibilities of circular walks based entirely within Coverdale.

It would not be entirely true to describe Coverdale as the undiscovered dale. There are plenty of people who know it and love it. It has, at Horsehouse and Carlton, two particularly charming villages and, for the discerning walker, great possibilities.

Between Coverdale and Walden lies a more familiar piece of territory, Pen Hill. Pen Hill dominates mid-Wensleydale. It is a typical Wensleydale hill, with all those features so perfectly described by the great Yorkshire geologist John Phillips when describing his Yoredale series of limestones in the 1830s. The long rambles and surveys taken by Phillips included most of the higher summits of Upper Wharfedale and Wensleydale including Pen Hill and led to his great work *The Geology of Yorkshire* published in 1836.

Pen Hill is quite superb. Climb it from West Witton, along the field path behind the village up to the old road from West Burton, going east to Pen Hill Farm on the Melmerby road and the track at the lane corner (where it is possible to leave a car if you do not want to walk the whole way) for the summit ridge and beacon. It is, naturally, a superb viewpoint, looking right into the Vale of Mowbray to the east, and across and up the dale with the neighbouring flat-topped summits of Addleborough and Yorburgh to the west, and, across the valley Wegber, Woodhall Greets and Stags Fell.

A right of way crosses from Black Scar, to the west of the ancient beacon, directly back to West Witton; but there is much to be said for walking the full ridge, perhaps picking up the path beyond Dove Scar that descends to West Burton, and a choice of ways around the side of the fell, none better in fact than the old, unsurfaced road, back to West Witton.

North of the river, the busy little market town of Leyburn

provides a useful focal point for mid-Wensleydale. At the time of writing at least, the two United Wensleydale bus services meet in Leyburn market-place and provide inter-connecting services, service 26 from Richmond which continues along the south side of the valley via Aysgarth and West Burton, to Hawes and service 127 from Ripon which operates via Redmire, Carperby and Askrigg. There is also service 78 to Bedale and Northallerton. These services enable a number of quite exciting and interesting walks on both sides of the river to be planned, perhaps returning to a parked car at Leyburn, or changing at Leyburn for Darlington or Ripon and Harrogate. Leyburn Station is used once or twice a year for Dales Rail services on the Wensleydale line from York.

A popular walk from Leyburn is the path behind Thornborough Hall up Leyburn Shawl, a splendid viewpoint associated, doubtless without shadow of evidence, with the recapture of Mary, Queen of Scots when she tried to escape from Castle Bolton. It was laid out, in the last century, as a promenade for the fashionable of Leyburn to stroll along. Paths continue from the Shawl towards Preston-under-Scar or Wensley, providing interesting circular or through-dale walks.

The moorlands behind Preston and Redmire are still full of evidence of the lead-mining industry, extremely significant, if not quite as dominant, in this part of Wensleydale as in Swaledale.

Any ramble north of the river is sooner or later drawn towards the eminence of Bolton Castle that most splendid and romantic of ruins. From Wensley an attractive walk through the parklands and woodlands of Bolton Park – home of the present Lord Bolton – leads to Redmire and obvious link paths to the village of Castle Bolton (an interesting reversion for a name) and the castle. The castle is open to the public most of the year and contains an excellent restaurant. Castle Bolton village church has, too, at most seasons of the year, an exhibition of local or topical interest for the attention of visitors.

There is insufficient space to do justice to the illustrious history of the castle, built in the late fourteenth century for the powerful Scrope family – the same Scropes that are mentioned in Shakespeare's *Henry IV*. Its most famous prisoner was, of course, Mary, Queen of Scots, held there from 13 July 1568 to 26 January 1569. That at least is documented fact, though romantic novelists and topographers have been dining out on Mary ever since. Its mixture of preserved portions and gaping, hollow ruin make it, in truth, the perfect setting for any Gothic tale; its huge presence on the hillside makes it a dominant landmark in Wensleydale for many miles around.

You can of course park at the little free car park at Castle Bolton with a choice of some good walks. The bridleway up the moor to Apedale leads to Swaledale, or you can return perhaps via Cobscar and Redmire pasture, or along the old county road (black dotted line on the map west of Castle Bolton but, yes, a public road through the fields) through Bolton Parks to Carperby, perhaps returning through West Bolton.

Aysgarth with its magnificent series of waterfalls is an obvious target from Castle Bolton, and there is a seven-mile circular walk between the Information Centre and Castle Bolton which a pamphlet on sale at the Information Centre describes in detail. One interesting feature on this route is the lost medieval village of Thoresby, down at Slapestone Wath ford, which is now no more than a series of grassy mounds.

Anyone exploring the Aysgarth area has, of course, the advantage of Arthur Gemmell's excellent Aysgarth Area Footpath Map on sale in most local shops. The clarity of detail on this map makes it simple for any walker to pick out a route of his choice and be certain that the stiles or gaps are where shown.

Any walk from Aysgarth will, of course, include the waterfalls at some stage – a geological display in the Information Centre gives insight into the combined effects of water and ice which, over millennia, have created the gigantic steps over the limestones that create the visual splendours of the upper, middle and lower falls.

A rather less well-known force a couple of miles downriver is Redmire Force, best reached on the south side of the river from Aysgarth via Hestholme, and along the lovely riverside path from Hestholme Bridge (now part of the Yoredale Way – see Chapter 13) which eventually plunges into thick woodland and descends to the immensely lovely shallow falls in a thickly wooded glade. You can follow this route right through to Wensley, or pick up the enclosed track from Wanlass (another county road), head for West Witton and a choice of high- and low-level ways back to Aysgarth. The eastern end of this walk is off both the Aysgarth Footpath Map and Sheet 98 OS map, so some juggling on the edges of maps is required, but it is a lovely walk.

A variation of this is to go across the field path to West Burton, one of the most photographed villages of the Dales, situated as it is in a quite perfect setting around its village green. To the north of the village, behind the old mill, is a beautiful, almost hidden waterfall, and careful pathfinding (see the Aysgarth Footpath Map) will enable you to climb up the hillside on a spectacular little path that eventually joins the old green way below Dove Scar, a quite breathtakingly beautiful panoramic walk around the end of the fell, with views along the whole of Wensleydale, before descending to join the old road to East Witton. A track northwards descends to the wood immediately to the west of the ruined foundations of the tiny chapel of the Knights Templar, a religious brotherhood, who built the chapel and ran a hospice here in the twelfth century. A few grave- and coffin-stones remain as a moving testimony to a way of life. From the main road below the chapel, the riverside path via Hestholme leads to Aysgarth Church.

West Burton lies, of course, in Walden, a little cul-de-sac valley of great loveliness, never more so than in late spring and early summer when the old meadows are ablaze with colour. There is a good valley bottom path right up to the head of the dale where the Walden road – in fact an almost indecipherable bridleway – will take you over the shoulder of Buckden Pike into Upper Wharfedale; or you can climb from Whiterow to Bradley or Horsehouse in Coverdale, or via Myers Gill to Newbiggin in Bishopdale.

If Walden's appeal lies in its quietness, the adjacent valley Bishopdale has the disadvantage of having the main B6160 road running through it, heavy with traffic and noise in the summer months. There are, nonetheless, pleasant footpaths up the valley sides, from Thoralby via Haw Sike to New House, then, on the other side of the gill, as far as Kidstone Pass at Dale Head. It is an interesting valley, with the deep valley basin – actually at one point lower than the main valley of the Ure, a unique geological phenomenon – often flooded after heavy rain when the ancient glacial lakes seem magically to reappear. Seekers after solitude are more likely to head for the higher passes, for example taking the bridleway up from Thoralby onto the Stake Allotment and perhaps returning via Carperly Green and Addleborough to Thornton Rust, where the recently modified footpath network now provides a good, direct route beyond Hawthorn Farm to the riverside path for Aysgarth.

There are excellent valley and riverside paths upriver to Askrigg from Aysgarth, most notably the one which goes by river or old railway below Woodhall to Thwaite Holme. It is always a matter of bitter regret that, in the late 1960s and early 1970s, the local authorities gave in to parochial pressures and self-interests and the old Wensleydale railway line offered to the county for a song as a footpath and bridleway was never acquired. It is difficult to forgive or forget such follies; as time goes by the loss will be ever more evident, particularly as the footpath close to the railway line itself, with its firm trackbed and elevated views, will inevitably cause people to trespass there and local farmers have the combined nuisance of an existing right of way and parallel track which no amount of warning notices and barbed wire will prevent people – local perhaps more than visitors – from using. Such folly cannot be pardoned.

You can return from Askrigg along a quite delightful path from the hamlet of Newbiggin climbing up to Heugh, then a high-level bridleway below Ivy Scar right through to Carperby; easy pleasant walking throughout and with quite extensive views.

Upper Wensleydale

The distinctive outlines of the township of Askrigg are now familiar – too familiar many local people would argue – to television viewers, and as a starting-point for some splendid local walks it is justifiably popular. It is, moreover, a village with some life – summer musical events in the church, the activities of the Askrigg Mill Foundation bringing disadvantaged young people from the cities to enjoy a stay in the countryside; there are signs of the village's outward-looking commitment to the world just over the seemingly infinite Wensleydale horizons.

One of the great little walks in the Dales is, of course, up Mill Gill – along the lane by the church north-westwards, then the path behind the old mill and up the steep gill to the magnificent little waterfall, visited and admired by Wordsworth among many others. You can follow the gill right up to Whitfield Gill, a steep, wooded ravine with a spectacular little waterfall. Changes in the footpath network to facilitate access up the gill are being planned, and clear signs and waymarks will indicate the route when changes are implemented. You can return to Askrigg by one of the more direct paths from the moorland track, above Whitfell Gill, Low Straits Lane, and, as Askrigg Church comes suddenly into view, you will begin to see the point about Wensleydale being a valley of subtle surprises.

The route from Askrigg to Hawes I would most commend is to keep your height to Helm and Skell Gill, and a lovely path just below the fell by Shaw Gill and Litherskew; this offers views all the way. You can follow the old railway line only as far as Cams House, but then must join this higher path below Litherskew. The fords across the river shown on the map are only negotiable in the driest weather.

Once again, there is an excellent Stile map to assist the rambler in the Hawes area, this time by Ralph Bradley, but with the same attention to detail and elucidation of awkward points for the walker as in other maps in the series.

Close to Aysgarth is Bainbridge, another of those stunningly beautiful Dales villages that finds its way into all the calendars. Bainbridge offers the ideal place to explore Raydale from, the valley of the little River Bain, and, of course, Semerwater. A well signposted and waymarked path leads from the top of the hill above Bainbridge above the narrow gorge of the Bain – reputedly the shortest river in England – descending to cross low fields to the edge of Semerwater.

Semerwater is one of the very few natural lakes in Yorkshire, a lake as rich in botanical, geological and natural history as it is in beauty. An Iron Age village once existed by its banks, doubtless giving the germ of the legend of the lake, the village sunk by a traveller's curse after he was offered neither meat nor drink. It is a pity, given its beauty and its scientific importance, that the lake has to bear such heavy recreational pressures with motor boats and waterskiing, activities more suitable for a popular seaside resort than a quiet lake in the heartland of a National Park, inevitably increasing the risk to a vulnerable habitat. It is to be hoped solutions can be found in the none too remote future.

The path to the east and south of the lake leads past the tiny ruined church of Stalling Busk, abandoned without ceremony in the early years of the present century when the villagers acquired a new and more convenient building, and now, with its unusual cottage windows, a melancholy and oddly moving ruin. From

Stalling Busk you can climb up to join the stony track which climbs over the Stake Pass into Wharfedale; or cross to Marsett and Raydale; or go up Bardale Beck right up and over to Bardale Head and Dodd Fell; or, from either Marsett or Countersett – with its many Quaker associations – onto Wether Fell and Yorburgh, and steep and splendid paths down to Gayle or Burtersett.

Wether Fell is, of course, crossed by the Roman road from Bainbridge, where remains of the small fort can still be seen as green and grassy mounds. The Roman road from Bainbridge is, in itself, an attractive walk, offering possibilities of attractive circular walks to and from Bainbridge.

And so to Hawes, the capital of upper Wensleydale. It is, in every sense, a fascinating town, a town of personality, of oddity, of charm. There is nowhere quite like it in England, an independent, no-nonsense place, where bureaucracy is simply not believed.

It is, of course, an important market town and on market day you will find it difficult to find a parking place, whilst bus users will find Hawes served by an amazing variety of services, including the special 800 services from West Yorkshire at weekends, Mr Whaite's service from Settle on Tuesdays and Saturdays in the summer months, the Ribble services from Kendal, and, of course, Dales Rail buses from Garsdale Station.

There is a National Park Information Centre in the old station building in the station yard, whilst the goods shed has been converted by the County Council into the Upper Dales Museum containing the magnificent collection of Dales bygones of Wensleydale historians and authors Marie Hartley and Joan Ingilby. Both information centre and the museum are well worth a visit.

You could find no better introduction to the town than the little Town Trail, on sale in the Centre and at local bookshops, which explains much of the history and the present character of the town and its twin, Gayle, with whom much friendly rivalry still exists. Hawes possesses perhaps the only bookshop in the world whose proprietor, Kit Calvert, the rescuer of the famous Wensleydale Cheese which is now manufactured in the town – trusts the customers so much that when you buy your book, you leave the cash in a tin.

Hawes owes much to men like Kit whose dogged determination to keep traditional ways and values alive, and generosity to the village, has helped the little township to keep its especial character and independence.

An obvious short walk from Hawes is to Hardraw to view the famous waterfall. You can get there along the Pennine Way, or perhaps with the help of the leaflet on sale at the National Park Information Centre, along field paths by Sedbusk and Simonstone. There is no right of way up to the force itself – you must go through the bar of the Green Dragon Hotel, paying a modest entrance fee, and then wandering into the natural amphitheatre to this most dramatic of Dales falls, at 99 feet reputedly the highest (above the surface) in England, a slender column of shimmering water that never ceases to delight, filling the air with spray.

It was always a major tourist attraction, never more so than when the excursion trains steamed into Hawes Station and allowed Victorian ladies, in their full skirts, to walk along the paved ways up to and around the splendid falls, doubtless getting their bonnets wet as they scrambled behind the falls to view the famous rainbow effects. The owner, the wealthy Lord Wharncliffe, laid out a whole series of ornamental, flagged paths, providing local employment and work for the quarries at a time of depression. Many of these are now overgrown, but you can still trace them, up to and around the falls, little staircases that are as Victorian as ferns, cast iron and steamboats.

Hardraw attracted crowds for, amongst other things, regular brass band contests. Happily the tradition has been revived, in spring of each year, with the natural amphitheatre cleaned out and restored to allow local bands to compete to the highest standards and something of the old spirit to be recaptured.

More ornamental walks exist in Shaw Gill Wood, above the waterfall, where the old paved ways have been repaired and a foot-bridge restored. This area is best reached from High Shaw, and is well worth exploration, keeping to the rights of way at either side of the gill.

To the north of Hawes is Stags Fell, an area riddled with quarry workings and stone mines. As the lead mines closed in the later years of the last century, some of the labour was absorbed by the quarrying industries around Hawes, on Stags Fell and in Burtersett, utilizing Hawes Station and the railway to East Lancashire and Manchester via the Lancashire and Yorkshire line. It is said that much of Victoria Station, Manchester, came from the Hawes quarries.

The technique of mining the stone, rather than working an extensive quarry face, was used a great deal, perhaps because the quarrymen, former miners, fully understood the techniques involved, and could work a face of good stone deep underground.

Abbotside Common, of which Stags Fell forms a part, is subject to an old access agreement allowing the public to wander freely on the fellside, away from the footpaths and bridleways; there is a restriction, however, on dogs, which cannot be allowed on the fell except on the public bridleway. There are extensive views from the fell edge, above Maze Holes, and the walker with a taste for wilderness can wander up to Lovely Seat right on the Muker Boundary, looking down onto the Buttertubs Pass.

On the far side of the Buttertubs road is Fossdale – undoubtedly the original site for Fors Abbey, and not near Askrigg as is sometimes supposed, before the community transferred to Jervaulx. The finding of a monk's grave, about a century ago, in Fossdale confirms this view. A popular walk from Hawes is to climb Shunner Fell, following the Pennine Way from Hardraw, a bleak, boggy summit, though with splendid views to compensate, returning down Hearne and the side of Fossdale to rejoin the Pennine Way above Hardraw. The bridleway that cuts around the shoulder of the fell to the west zigzags down into the hamlet of Cotterdale, another isolated and altogether enchanting little valley. The footpath then contours around below the fell and makes an attractive circular walk back to Hawes, or, with more time in hand, you might take the path by the forestry plantation climbing up to Cotter End, another fine viewpoint, to meet the ancient High Way along the fell edge from Hawes to Kirkby Stephen via Hell Gill, a most exciting walk. But if you have to return to Hawes, descend the path which crosses the High Way to the wood above Thwaite Bridge. Cross the main road past Thwaite House Farm to a stile up the fieldside to Mossdale Head where, just beyond the old railway line, there is a fine waterfall. The path goes along farmtracks and field paths past Birk Rigg, and then is a riverside path to Appersett for Hawes.

There is, of course, the old corpse way from Cotterdale over the top from the hamlet by Tarn Hill to High Dyke and down to the little church at Lunds, the nearest consecrated ground; but an awesome journey it must have been across the bleak and open fell.

The fells south of Hawes are easily reached for a day or even an afternoon's walk – Yorburgh via Gayle or Burtersett, Wetherfell perhaps via Duerley Beck and Sleddale, Ten End by the Pennine Way from Hawes, perhaps coming down the old Dodd Fell road. The next valley, Snaizeholme, has some interesting paths to explore, going as they do through the Mirk Pot Nature Reserve. Keep to footpaths if going through the reserve: visitors are always welcome, and Hugh Kemp, who runs the reserve and manages the forestry, takes a keen interest in local natural history. Anyone wishing to visit the reserve, particularly with a party, should write to him at Mirk Pot Farm, Snaizeholme, Hawes.

The next valley to carry yet another tributary of the Ure is Widdale, with the ancient road into Dentdale along the side of Widdale Fell.

But finally the Ure, now little more than a moorland beck, swings northwards under the shadow of Cotter End and Lunds Fell, finally vanishing to a tiny moorland sike graced by the name "River Ure" high up in the wet moorland.

I confess to a great affection for this top corner of Wensleydale; austere, even bleak landscapes meeting up with Garsdale Head. We are back in the epic landscapes, the brooding northern wilderness with more than a hint of Scandinavia, a Sibelius landscape where human influence and the softer aspects of human experience seem at best, only momentary. And for a valley as fine as Wensleydale, that is exactly how it should be.

REFERENCE

Maps

Ordnance Survey Landranger 1:50,000 Sheet 98 Wensleydale and Wharfedale; 99 Northallerton and Ripon

Ordnance Survey Outdoor Leisure 1:25,000 The Three Peaks

The Aysgarth and District Footpath Map, Arthur Gemmell (Stile Maps)

The Hawes and District Footpath Map, Ralph Bradley (Stile Maps)

Books

Walks in Wensleydale, Geoffrey Wright (Dalesman, 1977)
Walking in the Northern Dales, Ramblers' Association (Dalesman, 1973)
Walks Around Harrogate, Ramblers' Association (Harrogate Corporation, 1972)
Rambles Around Ripon, Ramblers' Association (Harrogate District Council 1979)
The Hawes Town Trail, Roger Stott (Author, 1980)
Under Wether Fell, James Alderson (Author, 1980)

11

Nidderdale

The River Nidd is not among the longer nor the more spectacular of Dales rivers; indeed except perhaps at Knaresborough I suspect few non-walkers have ever seen it, tucked away as it is down in the dale bottom away from the houses, the people and the cars.

But the real mystery about Nidderdale is that it was never included in the Yorkshire Dales National Park. Upper Nidderdale, upstream from Pateley, is as fine Dales country as any given special parliamentary protection, with great variety of landscape in a very small area, and much that is quite unique and very precious. Why it was never included doubtless was due to some murky political in-fighting which involved the Water Authorities and restrictions upon access; attitudes have now changed, but the National Park boundaries have not. Maybe the cynical, looking at the lovely unspoiled beauty of Ramsgill, or Middlesmoor or the high moors, would observe that Nidderdale gets on very nicely without the additional layers of bureaucracy of a National Park and it would be difficult to contradict this view until, perhaps, you discover how much better the footpaths are signposted and the stiles are maintained in the National Park area where these things receive a higher degree of priority.

It is not a difficult dale to reach. Its focal point is Pateley Bridge, a pleasant, bustling little town, which, if it has not the attractiveness of a Grassington or Hawes, enjoys a lovely hillside site which in Italy no doubt would be full of terraced gardens and vineyards. A good bus service, West Yorkshire Service 24, links Harrogate with Pateley, not along the main road north of the river, but linking the major villages, Hampsthwaite, Birstwith, Darley, to the south, or, occasionally, via Markington. There are some through buses from West Yorkshire at weekends, but north of Pateley the service is far less frequent. It is worth checking in the timetable because the riverside paths in Nidderdale are so

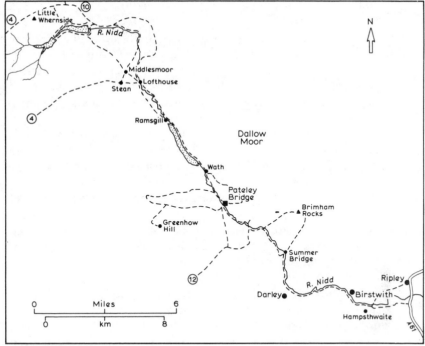

NIDDERDALE

superb, that if you can time your bus to collect you and take you back home or to a parked car, it offers delightful possibilities. But there are plenty of opportunities for circular walks, perhaps using a bit of riverside for part of the way, before or after climbing up one of the steep edges.

But let us begin with the riverside path. You could, of course, follow it right up from Knaresborough through the attractively wooded Bilton Banks, but inevitably it then becomes mixed up with the interminable suburbs of Harrogate which hardly evoke the atmosphere for a romantic Dales walk. Better to start at either Ripley or Killinghall, Ripley because it is an estate village of extraordinary charm and beauty (the castle is of great historic interest, but you will need longer time to explore it than can be spared on a walk), it is on the regular 36 Ripon bus from Harrogate and has a very pleasant connecting route to the river; Killinghall because the Nidderdale bus goes through the village *en route* to Harrogate and that could be convenient if you plan to catch it from Dacre, Summer Bridge or even Pateley back to a parked car.

From Ripley an enclosed way goes over the little bridge in front of the castle, (you will discover this part of Nidderdale suffers, like Swaledale, from the edge of the map problem), to Clint from where there is a field path to Hampsthwaite; a fairly easy to find path from Killinghall by Crag Hill Farm also emerges near Hampsthwaite Church.

From Hampsthwaite there is a mixture of field path and road, and then riverside to Birstwith with its mill; riverside again beyond Birstwith, by New Bridge, a most elegant little pack-horse bridge. You cannot get beyond Hartwith Mill Bridge without trespassing except to walk along the road, but a better section of riverside path starts opposite the Holme, by the old Darley Station on the greatly lamented Nidderdale railway which ran from Harrogate to Pateley, and which remained open, at least for freight, until the 1960s.

Between Darley and Summer Bridge is an excellent section of riverside path, though railway enthusiasts might be tempted to take the section of path by the old railway. Summer Bridge is a good point to pick up the Harrogate bus if time presses, which would in a way be a pity, because the section of path from Summer Bridge to Pateley is even finer, starting by the wood yard at Summer Bridge and going along a track which eventually gives access to the riverside path, again a lovely winding section of quite secluded river to Glasshouses, where you must cross to follow the opposite bank along a woodland track, just below the old railway line, into Pateley Bridge.

This is all very good, very pleasant walking throughout, with no real difficulty in path finding. The existence of the bus service along the main road makes it easy to leave the path at any appropriate point, though if you are using a car, there is much to be said for timing the walk to use the bus on the outward trip and walking back to the car to save worrying about timekeeping or timetables.

For a circular walk involving a major tourist attraction, leave the bus or car in either Summer Bridge or Glasshouses, and take one of the winding paths or tracks up to Brimham Rocks; from Glasshouses via Wilsill, White Houses and High Woods, from Summer Bridge via Hazel Bank and the path above Smelt Houses, onto Brimham Moor for Brimham Rocks.

Brimham Rocks, now a National Trust property, are a collection of wind-carved gritstone crags, worn into quite fantastic shapes and often with equally fantastic names. It is a fascinating area to wander around, scrambling between the gaunt shapes, some like huge petrified mushrooms, others like ancient beasts, the whole area overlooking the Nidderdale escarpment and full of atmosphere, especially in late summer with the heather richly purple and the many rowan trees an intense scarlet against the warm grey-brown stone.

There is, in fact, ample car-parking at the rocks, and an excellent National Trust Information Centre and shop to cater for visitors' needs. The area can be extremely busy on Sunday afternoons.

With careful planning you can descend to the riverside and return to your starting-point with a section of riverside path to make a circular walk.

Almost as impressive, over on the other side of the valley, are Guise Cliff and Yorke's Folly. Reach them from Pateley climbing up past Bewerley and the path that cuts off the zigzag of the road by Strikes Farm to join the path along the edge of the escarpment, which brings you to the strange towers of Yorke's Folly, a typical nineteenth-century Gothic mock ruin built by a local landowner to keep men employed and add a little interest to the view. It is, undoubtedly, a thrilling viewpoint, across to Brimham Rocks, Pateley and the higher dale.

A choice of ways down, none better than the route through Hawkshaw Gill Wood and riverside path back to Pateley, or forward to Summer Bridge.

Pateley Bridge is, of course, a convenient centre for a wide variety of walks, and is well supplied with car parks, cafés, pubs and other facilities for visitors, including an excellent little local folk museum.

A favourite short circular walk is to take the Harrogate road to the start of the "Panorama Walk" a steep path, left, by the cemetery – cut across, left, part way up the hill to the ruined church of Old St Mary, a seventeenth-century church like the one at Stalling Busk, abandoned and covered with ivy. An old parishioners' way leads through a little gate back to Panorama Walk which, as its name implies, give attractive views over the valley as you climb up to Knott Side.

Take the bridleway north at Knott to the lane, turning left to the road from Pateley; almost directly ahead a stile leads to a path through the edge of extensive sandstone quarries, Scot Gate Ash Quarry from where much excellent building stone came which was exported by the railway which it reached by means of a series of extraordinary ramps down the hillside.

This path joins Wath Lane, a lovely sloping lane down to the charming hamlet of Wath giving extensive views up the dale; return to Pateley along the riverside and raised trackbed of the Nidderdale Light Railway.

The little standard-gauge railway line was originally built to transport materials for the building of Angram Reservoir and was opened between Pateley Bridge and Lofthouse in 1907 and remained open for passengers until 1930, and freight until 1936 whilst Scar House Reservoir was being completed.

You can now, in fact, follow the old trackbed up the valley as a footpath for most of the way, with the right of way on or close to the old permanent way. The path from Wath round the back of Gouthwaite Reservoir, now an important nature reserve and bird sanctuary, leads to Bouthwaite for Ramsgill, where you must leave the line whichever path you take on either side of the valley to Lofthouse.

At Lofthouse, however, you can see the old station building with its cast-iron pillars and station platforms and old toilets still in commission. Beyond Lofthouse the present reservoir road follows the line right up to the reservoirs, passing the bricked-up tunnel close to Goyden Pot where the railway line ran through the cliff side, and, if you look carefully at the north side of Scar House Reservoir, sections of sleepers are still in evidence.

Like Grassington, Pateley Bridge was once a thriving lead-mining town. No clearer evidence of the importance of this industry in Nidderdale can be obtained than a walk up Foster Beck, just to the north-west of Pateley. Foster Beck Mill, with its huge thirty-five foot water-wheel, was a hemp mill but is now an inn, and although the wheel is no longer in working order, its existence is a graphic reminder of the importance of water-power for industry in the Pennines.

The track up the gill is dominated by caravan sites which soon give way to a fine wooded dale; keep to the left where the track forks at Westfield, and you are soon entering a landscape dominated by the remains of lead workings. Notable amongst these are the remains of Prosperous Mill, which last saw service in 1872. The flue is still visible on the hillside. Several levels or mine entrances are evident; avoid entering or going too close to these old workings – many are dangerous.

The bridleway climbs up past Near Hardcastle and Bradstone Beck to Greenhow, that remote, bleak little mining village lost in an almost Klondike atmosphere of semi-derelict farms, spoil tips, old workings, a redundant church and The Miners' Arms, an area fascinating for industrial archaeologists. Greenhow is, for much of the year, swathed in mist and rain, acting as it does as a major meteorological barrier between the west and east of the Pennines. It can be pouring with rain in Grassington and sunny in Pateley; sunny in Grassington but pouring in Pateley, depending on the mood of the weather. But whatever is happening on either side, Greenhow seems to get the worst of it.

Whilst the energetic can cross Greenhow perhaps via Stump Cross to Grimwith or via Skyreholme into Wharfedale, the easiest way back to Pateley is along the old miners' tracks via Sun Side, Hole Bottom and Ladies Riggs direct into the village, a satisfying descent to a softer and more civilized valley world.

Upper Nidderdale does, indeed, provide fell walking of a challenging and rewarding nature. If from Pateley you follow lane or path up onto Brownstay Ridge, keeping on the Kirkby Malzeard lane, you can cross the moor where the lane is unenclosed, following the open fell over Low Carle Edge, behind High Buckle to Far Hill, keeping your height beyond Jordan Crag and across Fountains Earth Moor past the great rocks known as Jenny Twig and her daughter Tib to join the Colsterdale road for Lofthouse. This is rough, wild walking, not for the uninitiated, requiring strong boots, strong lungs and a good compass, often crossing very rough terrain, but for the true moorland tramper and bog-trotter, vintage stuff.

The top end of Nidderdale is, by anyone's standards, superb. In terms of landscape heritage everything north of Patelely Bridge is of National Park standard; the highest part of the dale, north of Lofthouse, is quite magnificent.

If Lofthouse is a village of considerable charm, its near neighbour, Middlesmoor is that very rare phenomenon in the Pennines, a hill village, the kind of settlement not uncommon in Mediterranean countries, perched high on a conical hill or, as

Middlesmoor, clinging to the edge of a ridge. You expect red pantiles and stucco instead of grey stone and Yorkshire slate, there, high up on the hillside. And on one side of the village is the steep gorge of the Nidd on its final journey to the high reservoirs, on the other the astonishing gorges of How Stean, deep limestone caverns and overhangs.

There are many attractive combinations of walks in this compact but fascinating little area. Do not take a car up to Middlesmoor – there is little room for parking and such a magnificent setting deserves due homage paid to it by a pilgrimage on foot, its little church a marvellous landmark from whatever direction you approach.

There are still some weekend buses as far as Lofthouse, but if you are looking for a car park, a convenient one exists at Stean corner, just across the bridge from Lofthouse, where you can leave a vehicle for a small charge. Explore the gorge and little cave (modest entrance fee – pay at the café) then follow the lane towards Stean hamlet before picking up the signposted path back over How Stean Beck which climbs up to Middlesmoor.

From Middlesmoor you might take the track direct over Rain Stang to Scar House Reservoir, or leave it for the track by Northside Head and a field path down to Limley where close to the footpath, you can reach Manchester Hole and Goyden Pot, two celebrated Nidderdale pot-holes. Go back down the valley by one of the riverside paths. Or you might make for Low Woodale or New Houses, and take the moorland track up to The Edge, perhaps climbing up Bracken Ridge right up to Potts Moor. This is one of those splendid little high-level routes which, for modest effort, is so very rewarding; you can follow the moorland track right round across Lofthouse Moor to the castellated shooting-lodge, behind which a little pony track cuts down by the wood to Thrope Farm and a lovely green valley track to Lofthouse; else keep your height for the Lofthouse road and descend directly into the village.

The road from Lofthouse up to Scar House is a private one, but open as a toll road for most of the year for motorists as far as the reservoir. It has pleasant lay-bys and picnic places, and you can enjoy an extremely pleasant stroll, requiring about an hour, crossing the dam, following the track and old railway line right around Scar House Reservoir up to Angram Reservoir Dam before returning back down the other side of Scar House; like Gouthwaite this is an interesting area for ornithologists.

More energetic souls who have worked out the logistics of transport, accommodation or backpacking can, of course, utilize a number of the major inter-valley routes that converge at the head of Nidderdale. In days of pedlars and pack-ponies, Nidderdale was, in effect, a strategic crossroads of the Dales, and the network of ancient pack-horse ways at the dalehead reflect this. You can cross to Colsterdale, Coverdale, across Little Whernside to Kettlewell, and up that strange and forbidding peak – surely the least climbed of all the higher summits – Meugher, descending over Grassington Moor to Yarnbury and Grassington. Indeed with care – see Geoffrey White's valuable *Walks in Nidderdale* – you can plan very rewarding ascents of Little and Great Whernside and Meugher from Scar House and Stean respectively, and for most people this is probably the best way of doing them from the Nidderdale side. But do not expect this to be easy walking; this is amongst the wildest, the loneliest and toughest fell-walking country in England, and whilst it may attract some people for that very reason, it is not to be tackled lightly or without the considerable respect it deserves.

REFERENCE

Maps

Ordnance Survey Landranger 1:50,000 Sheet 98 Wensleydale and Wharfedale; 99 Northallerton and Ripon; 104 Leeds and Bradford

Ordnance Survey 1:25,000 Second Series Sheets SE 05/15, SE 06/16, SE 07/17

Books

Walks in Nidderdale, Geoffrey White (Dalesman, 1979)

Walks for Motorists in the Yorkshire Dales, Ramblers' Association (Warne, 1980)

Nidderdale, Pateley Bridge WEA Class – Ed. Jennings (WEA, 1967)

Walks in Nidderdale (Nidderdale Society, Pateley Bridge, 1981)

12

Washburndale

With Washburndale has our wheel of the Dales come full circle. We are back into the countryside on the fringe of West Yorkshire's towns, the lung (and indeed the water supply) of Leeds, known, loved and tramped by so many generations of ramblers from the dark streets and the satanic mills that there seems to be a presence, an awareness on those river-bottom paths of the passage of boots, of knapsacks.

Older ramblers mingle their memories of the Washburn with those of trams to White Cross and Sammy Ledgard's buses that rocked and swayed over the back of the Chevin down to Otley, at a fare of coppers, from where, for the strong of wind and stout of heart, the entire Washburn lay before you.

The Washburn is, in fact, a tributary of the Wharfe, coming down from the high moors by Barden Fell and Greenhow, through a long string of reservoirs, Thruscross, Fewston, Swinsty and Lindley Wood – Yorkshire's Lake District – before joining the Wharfe south of Leathley, opposite that other small paradise for ramblers, Otley Chevin.

It is not all that easy to reach by public transport. Apart from the odd market-day bus through Timble and Fewston, and buses out to the Menwith Hill camps from Harrogate, it is often a question of walking from Otley, Pool or Harrogate, making a fairly long day of it. Motorists, however, can enjoy opportunities to complete short circular walks from a number of possible parking places, most notably by the verge above Lindley Wood Reservoir, above Swinsty Reservoir, and the large public car park south of Thruscross Reservoir.

But maybe because you have got to walk a mile or two from the nearest bus to get into Washburn, it has attracted walkers out for a longer day's walk, crossing the high moors from the valley to

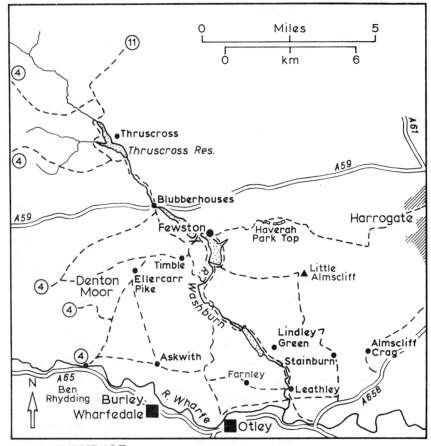

WASHBURNDALE

pick up transport home from one of the other major dales with lines of communication, west to the Wharfe and buses and trains from Ben Rhydding and Ilkley, north to the Nidd for Harrogate – Pateley buses and eastwards to Harrogate and buses along the Pool-Bradford road.

Pool, is, in fact, rather more than Otley, a way into Washburn. If you are coming from the Leeds direction you can alight from the bus at Bramhope Church, cross to the little Cromwellian Chapel, and down Staircase Lane – an ancient road – into Pool, served by Bradford–Harrogate buses. A field path from Pool Bridge links to a direct path to Leathley, a most attractive village with a church dating from Saxon times. The Washburndale path begins just behind Leathley Mill, following the mill go up to the bridge carrying the road from Farnley. It then becomes a most pleasant track and green way past a cottage and alongside Lindley Wood Reservoir; you walk, in fact between the aforesaid Lindley Wood and the reservoir, and it is a most attractive walk with level woods on one side and mirror-still water on the other.

At Lindley Bridge cross to the other side of the bridge to follow the track up alongside the continuation of the reservoir, before crossing back over a bridge and up to Dob Park Bridge.

This lovely little pack-horse bridge among the trees is a favourite among walkers – for very good reason. It carries, indeed, the most direct route back to Otley, along the track by Middle Farm and the main road to Newall, though a variation through the village of Clifton will offer some pleasant field paths into Otley; or you might cut across to Askwith, an extremely delightful path, using the Burley stepping-stones, although after heavy rain the only safe crossing of the river is at Ben Rhydding Bridge.

But to return to Dob Park Bridge. You can follow the track up from the bridge to the Farnley road and then across to Folly Hall, a farmhouse which for many years was a veritable ramblers' mecca under the hospitality of the legendary Mrs Dibbs with her pots of tea. The folly is, in fact, Dobpark Castle, another mock-Gothic ruin, visible across the valley.

Beyond Folly Hall the path descends to the river and the reservoir track up to Swinsty Dam.

On the other side of the river from Dob Park Bridge paths go up to Ellers Wood and along the other bank of the river or to Low Snowden and to Timble Gill, crossed by a splendid little hump-back bridge, built to commemorate the late Alderman Arthur Adamson, by the West Riding Ramblers' Association whose Honorary Secretary he was for many years. The stonework of the bridge was undertaken by Harry Saynor, doyen of ramblers and himself a Vice-President of the West Riding Ramblers' Association.

From the Adamson Bridge, a path climbs up the lane leading into Timble where the Timble Inn is well accustomed to looking after the needs of walkers. It is an interesting village, with a network of paths radiating from it. The back lane reached from Timble Beck forks back down to Swinsty Hall, a magnificent

Tudor (1570) and Jacobean house, in a beautiful setting in the woods close to Swinsty Reservoir.

Swinsty Reservoir, whilst lacking the charm of Lindley Wood, is an extremely pleasant place to stroll around. Its reservoir track adjoining the lane to and from Fewston makes it an ideal place to take a push-chair, pram or wheelchair from a car parked any-where on the quiet verge on the back lane, around the reservoir, across the dam of Fewston Reservoir, through Fewston village with its lovely late-seventeenth-century church, and back to the reservoir side.

There are a number of quite interesting options to get to or from Fewston and the transport links to and from Harrogate. The most satisfying, perhaps, is to take the footpaths through Haverah Park, starting from behind the Sun Inn, easily reached by lane or woodland path from Fewston. The track behind the Sun Inn leads to the path by John of Gaunt's Castle and Beaver Dyke Reservoir, right through Haverah Park to either Pot Bridge or Beckwithshaw depending on which route is chosen, from where there are delightful paths through the oak-woods by Oak Beck to Harlow Hill and the woodlands leading into the Valley Gardens and the centre of Harrogate.

The footpaths through Haverah Park will be forever linked with the name of Corrie Gaunt, a latter-day William Cobbett whose tireless energy and persistence with the former Claro Water Board and the West Riding County Council, and gather-ing of evidence from as far back as the fourteenth century and from octogenarians in the area, resulted in a famous legal victory at Quarter Sessions. When you wander along the footpaths of Haverah Park recall the effort and vigilance of Corrie Gaunt, the triumph of one individual against the ineptitude of officialdom.

It is possible, without undue difficulty, to return back towards Pool perhaps via Norwood Edge (with its notable wireless mast) and Little Almscliff Crag, before picking up the moorland track across Stainburn Moor, through West End across West Beck to Stainburn, a fascinating little hamlet set amid a spider's web of deep sunken lanes and old paths, continuing down East Beck to the little Riffa Wood, with its paved causeway deep in the wood leading down to Riffa Beck and Leathley. A choice of paths leads to the main Pool road, or indeed by path and lane you can easily reach Weeton Station on the Leeds–Harrogate railway.

Whilst it is only on the fringe of Washburndale, Almscliff Crag deserves space in any book on the Dales; you can reach it from any of the paths outlined above from Stainburn, or by field path from Weeton Station and Huby (an excellent afternoon's walk is to alight from the train at Weeton, take in Almscliff before making your way to North Rigton and Horn Farm to Pannal Station).

Almscliff Crag is one of those curious little islands of projecting wind-carved gritstone, doubtless a small peak which projected above the last great Ice Age glacier which smoothed and flattened the surrounding landscape, leaving this stark little cluster of gritstone, a kind of miniature Brimham Rocks. It is a splendid area to wander round and scramble over, with narrow passages to squeeze through, boulders to climb on. Children delight in it; it is also famed as a nursery slope for somewhat older noviciates in rock climbing. It is also a stunning viewpoint, looking back across the Pennines, and Wharfedale or across the Vale of York – on a clear day you can distinguish the minster itself gleaming against the horizon.

But to return to the Washburn, Fewston and Timble. If your route out of the valley is to the west, some spectacular walking awaits you, again countryside well documented and well worn by generations of ramblers, but still somewhat bleak and forbidding in poorish weather, with few landmarks if once you lose your direction; compasses are essential in whatever conditions.

A classic route from Timble is along the forestry track by Sourby Farm and then up to Ellercar Pike and over the edge of Askwith Moor cutting across by the eastern edge of Moor Plantation to Moorside and Denton. Or you might go from Ellercarr Pike along the ancient packman's way, High Badgergate to the shooting-lodge at Crow Fell down to Denton. For some really grand moorland walking follow the track through the forest at Timble Ings, climbing up to Lippersley Pike along the ridge, another fine viewpoint, over Stainforth Gill and Gawkhill, coming back along the line of the Roman road, an almost indecipherable road which is yet in exact alignment with the modern A59 up from Blubber-houses. This intersects the path over Blubberhouses Moor from Raven's Peak back to Gill Beck and Timble.

Or, with a long afternoon before you, go from Lippersley across to Bow Shaw above March Ghyll Reservoir, over the Round Hill on Middleton Moor, to Langbar Moor for Beamsley

Beacon and Addingham, and transport back down Wharfedale.
It is essential to have 2½″ Ordnance maps to explore this area.
As they are First Series maps, they do not contain rights of way
which will need to be transferred from 1:50,000 sheets, though
sooner or later Second Series maps, with full footpath information will be on the market.

But what of Washburndale north of Timble? The continuation
of the valley path is through the thick woodland marked on the
map as Beecroft Moor Plantation where a path goes north-north-
westwards right up to Blubberhouses, at the head of Fewston
Reservoir.

Blubberhouses, a scattered Norse settlement on the A59,
among the fir trees and reservoirs, has few facilities, though there
is a shop on the Pateley road. This is, in fact, the way northwards,
following the road for a quarter of a mile uphill, before a track
(signposted) bears left, soon dropping down through woodlands
to a foot-bridge and, in a narrow and romantic gorge, climbing up
to the reservoir dam.

I must have been one of the very last people to walk up this
valley before the bulldozers and earth-movers finally obliterated
the top end of the path to build the dam. They were already in
action tearing up the trees to make space for a thirsty city's supply
of water.

More than a footpath vanished when the new Leeds Corporation Reservoir was built at Thruscross in the 1960s. An entire
village, West End, disappeared from the map – mill and churchyard, tiny inn and cottages. Halliwell Sutcliffe, writing in his
loquacious style in *The Striding Dales* of 1931, has a long and
melancholy panegyric on the subject of the "lost hamlet" of West
End. I explored it too, just before the reservoir builders moved in,
and it was a beautiful if melancholy place. It is very much more
lost now than in poor Sutcliffe's day, no more than a memory,
though a neat row of stone-built bungalows, on the crossroads by
the Stone House Inn up above the reservoir, now replaces the
hamlet and rehouses those who needed to be rehoused.

There is a good footpath round the top edge of the reservoir,
climbing up to Roundell's Allotment, and then presenting a
choice of connecting ways down to Darley or Dacre Banks in
Nidderdale. There is also the old road over Pockstone Moor via
Hey Slack, which curves around the Barden Fell, emerging at

Skyreholme and Appletreewick (a fine walk but keep to the track and avoid walking over the open moor where there are still unexploded shells).

An obvious route over the fine expanse of Barden Fell and Rocking Moor is to follow the Dales Way link from Harrogate which, in effect, goes via Haverah Park to Fewston, Timble and Blubberhouses, along the Washburn to the Thruscross Dam, and then via Burnt House and Spittle Ings, before crossing into the access area up to Rocking Stone, a large boulder which allegedly rocks, and Rocking Hall, a shooting-lodge. From here tracks lead over Long Ridge down to the deer park and Bolton Abbey. Remember from Spittle Ings westwards is part of the Barden Fell Access Area and subject to by-laws which include limitation on dogs and closure of the fell during shooting days or at time of fire risk.

You can, of course, make a circular walk including this back to Thruscross via Bramley Head and Lane Bottom – attractive moor edge country, all hawthorns and rowans, with, in late summer, a magnificent purple back-cloth of heather moor.

A more direct route to Wharfedale from Spittle Ings is to take the public path over Kex Gill, following the open moorland to Black Hill and Maiden Kirk to Hazelwood, and the track down Kex Gill Beck to Deerstones for Beamsley, Bolton Bridge and Addingham. All interesting, varied walking.

And finally, you might leave the Washburn northwards, over Hoodstroth Allotment and Humberstone Bank, crossing from High House Farm a dreary and rather featureless waste, mostly bent and rushes, down by Raven's Nest into Bewerley, the sudden contrast from the relative lushness of Nidderdale, reward enough.

REFERENCE

Maps
Ordnance Survey Landranger 1:50,000 Sheet 99 Northallerton and Ripon; 104 Leeds and Bradford
Ordnance Survey 1:25,000 First Series Sheets SE14, SE15, SE25
Ordnance Survey 1:25,000 Second Series Sheet SE24/34 Harewood

The Otley Footpath Map, Arthur Gemmell (Stile Maps)
Walking Washburn Way, Map and Guide (Ramblers' Association,
   1984)

Books
Walks for Motorists in the Yorkshire Dales, Ramblers' Association
   (Warne, 1980)
Walks in Lower Wharfedale, Geoffrey White (Dalesman, 1980)

13

Long-Distance Paths

Long-distance footpath walking is a relatively new phenomenon. People went on "walking tours" of course right from the early days of the Romantics. But following one particular route, a trail, is something quite different. It might, of course, be compared with a medieval pilgrimage, and, if Geoffrey Chaucer is to be believed, may have a similar cause, for did not he note when, in the spring

> . . . smale fowles maken melodye . . .
> Than longen folk to goon on pilgrimages.

Not in present times in search of a saint's shrine, but, following the star of Stephenson, Wainwright *et al.* along a well-worn and well-documented way.

And like the medieval pilgrims' paths, the modern long-distance paths have their inns and taverns, their company and their hardships, their difficulties and their rewards to enrich the lives of the modern pilgrim, within the Yorkshire Dales as else-where.

What is it about a long-distance path that makes such an appeal to late twentieth-century man?

In essence it is a romantic appeal, an age-old delight in dis-covering what lies just beyond that far horizon, what tomorrow will bring. You may like to know where you are going to spend the night, or you may trust to luck and what you find available. Both possibilities offer the delights of anticipation, the pleasant tension of a degree of uncertainty. It is good, too, to be totally independent of any mechanical contraption, to measure yourself against a substantial distance: "I walked there" is, in an age of instant mobility, no mean boast. It is an age-old primitive wan-

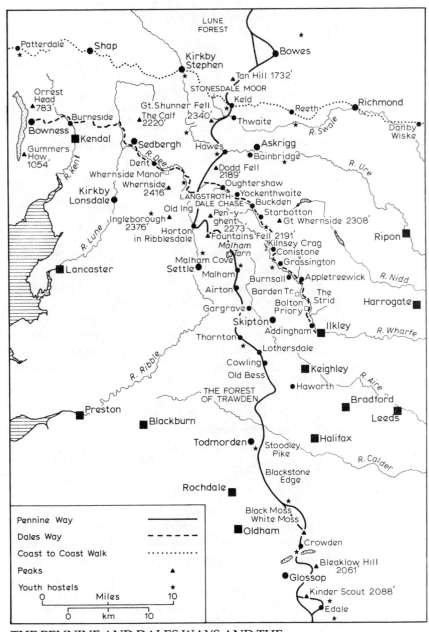

THE PENNINE AND DALES WAYS AND THE
COAST TO COAST WALK

derlust, the illusion of freedom, of the open road, a pleasure as acute for us as it was for our migrating ancestors crossing the primeval forests and forbidding wastes of Europe.

And, in more practical terms, it is a remarkably excellent and inexpensive way of seeing the Dales or any other countryside. Long-distance walkers have in the Dales splendid hospitality available at small guest-houses, farmhouses and country inns at still reasonable costs. The Ramblers' Association offer an invaluable *Bed, Breakfast and Bus* guide for around 80p (free to members) which lists addresses from all over England and which are coded if they serve any of the major long-distance paths such as the Pennine Way, the Coast to Coast Walk and the Dales Way in the Yorkshire Dales.

The cult of the long-distance footpath in Britain really began with the Pennine Way and the vision, courage and determination of one man, Tom Stephenson. In 1935 Tom, then a journalist on the *Daily Herald*, wrote an article called "Wanted a Long Green Trail" in response to a request from two American girls who, having walked the Appalachian Way in the United States asked if there was a similar route in England. Tom suggested a route from Derbyshire, through the Yorkshire Pennines and into Durham and Tynedale for the Cheviots and the Scottish Border. "None could walk that Pennine Way", he wrote, "without being improved in mind and body and inspired and invigorated and filled with the desire to explore every corner of this lovely island."

The war years prevented any progress on this noble idea. But following the reports of John Dower in 1944, and the Hobhouse Committee in 1947, the National Parks and Access to the Countryside Act of 1949 gave specific powers to the new National Parks Commission to set up long-distance footpaths, with generous grants for their creation and maintenance which included powers to operate ferry services should long-distance paths have to cross stretches of water – such was the enthusiasm of the early countryside legislators.

In practice it took sixteen long years from the passing of the 1949 Act to the official opening of the Pennine Way in spring 1965 – significantly the opening ceremony was held at Malham in the Yorkshire Dales. The reasons for the delay were more than just bureaucratic inertia. Farmers and landowners were genuinely concerned that the new provision would mean hordes of ill-controlled hikers crossing their land, damaging crops, smashing fences and leaving litter. Some fought to the bitter end, until the dreaded spectre of compulsory powers had to be brought before them. But finally the last piece of red tape was cut, the path opened, and literally hundreds of thousands of people have used the route.

The Pennine Way is still a remarkable physical challenge, 250 miles of wild, upland countryside, often going through deep bogs and ravines, steep hillsides and across barren wastes, a test of mental and physical endurance that attracts refugees from modern industrial civilization in their thousands.

There are just over sixty miles of Pennine Way in the Yorkshire Dales, or more precisely between Gargrave and Stainmore. It therefore provides a remarkably good south–north crossing of the region along a footpath which is very well defined, well signposted and with facilities along the way. With careful planning, either with the use of two cars or (preferably) with the use of local transport, it can be walked in day or weekend stages and for those of us with the kind of lives that cannot allow us to take two and a half or more weeks away from work, wives (or husbands) and worry, that might be the only feasible alternative. More to the point, the Pennine Way through the Yorkshire Dales really does contain some of the route's most spectacular and most satisfying stretches.

The way is very well waymarked, and very detailed guides are available to make any detailed description here unnecessary. But as an appetizer, it is worth while to list the contrasting sections of the route in the Dales.

From Gargrave to Malham the way goes through some of the greenest and most fertile countryside of its entire length, from the rolling Craven drumlins around Gargrave, to a gentle, even uncharacteristic, stretch of Pennine Way through soft pastures and meadows by the infant Aire from Newfield to Airton and Hanlith to Malham.

Malham is the start of the real mountain limestone country, with the Pennine Way using the tourist path from the village to the cove; it then climbs up to the high limestone plateau with the rocky pavements and short springy turf to the shores of the limpid tarn. Then another contrast, north of the tarn, as the way ascends Fountains Fell, a grim, peaty whaleback of a hill, dwarfing humankind as the wayfarer battles up a path through the peat onto a bleak and empty summit; but the views are superb. Pen y Ghent follows, one of the most dramatic peaks of the North of England, its craggy nose giving the impression of an authentic mountain: Ribblesdale blighted and austere below. You descend into the heart of the pot-hole country, with both Hull and Hunt Pot close to the path and worth time for a deviation. Then northwards, the way follows old stony ways and green tracks, across Ling Gill, up Cam Fell, into the wildest country in all England, over Ten End, Dodd Fell, before descending into Gayle and the fascinating little township of Hawes.

The crossing from Wensleydale to Swaledale has what every long-distance path needs, a touch of the epic, from Hardraw, with its long, shimmering waterfall, up the long, slow climb to Abbotside Common and onto the soggy summit of Shunnor Fell, again a splendid viewpoint on a clear day, a strange and weird place to be in mist or rain with the path vanishing in deep bog and morass.

The reward lies in the descent into Swaledale, a kind of early vision of paradise, as green and fertile as the summit of Shunnor is brown and bleak. From the hamlet of Thwaite with its celebrated Kearton Guest-House and Restaurant, the Pennine Way enters a little valley of incomparable beauty – a panoramic walk along the side of Kisdon, with its steep sides and waterfalls at Kisdon Force and East Gill, just below the hamlet of Keld.

From Keld the way re-enters no man's land – Wainwright's "rising featureless moorland" like a kind of latter-day test of the spiritual toughness, let alone the feet, of modern Pilgrims making any Progress. Tan Hill Inn offers a little comfort, only if you are fortunate enough, that is, to get there at opening times. The wastes of Sleightholme Moor follow, down to Sleightholme. Ahead Stainmore, and the moors to Teesdale.

But that is another region to explore.

To a certain degree the pessimists have been proved right. The Pennine Way has brought broad, eroded paths especially where the ground is boggy or peaty, orange peel, coke cans (a recent development is the can pull-ring that gets almost anywhere and seems to survive indefinitely). On a few busy periods in spring and early summer you can indeed see young people, mostly but not entirely male and in their twenties, "backpacking" along the way, often going in waves or more correctly strings of a dozen or more depending on which hostel, or campsite or farmhouse they have stayed in overnight.

Not surprisingly such minor examples of pollution and erosion cause a certain type of planner or more élitist mountaineer, to deplore the success and popularity of the "big name" routes, suggesting, indeed, that the very designation of a long-distance path will destroy the solitude, the challenge, the spiritual loneliness the original creators intended. And indeed, worst of all, cause massive bills to be paid for their maintenance (i.e. about the same as for a couple of miles of motorway verge). Such views require some historical perspective. Even at its maximum usage, the Pennine Way carries a fraction of the traffic many similar tracks and ways carried before the human species (in these islands at least) took to whizzing up and down in their cars along the motorways. Deep grooves and scars in the hillside, long grassed over and healed, are testimony to the capacity of the land to return to vegetation after less than a generation, which, in geological time, is less than a blink of an eyelid. It is still a revelation to some people to realize that footpaths, like roads, need to be maintained from the public purse, whether you use professional roadmen, voluntary labour or machines for the purpose. The true seeker for solitude is not forced to walk the Pennine Way. There are hundreds of square miles of empty uplands throughout the northern half of Britain where he can seek perfect solitude even in the late twentieth century, or perhaps even more so in the twentieth century after many decades of rural depopulation.

For in essence, a long-distance footpath is a packaged walking holiday. Your guidebook offers you an itinerary, a recommended route or more accurately a series of interlinked routes. It is selected by a person of local knowledge and insight, put together as a whole, interpreted for the walker. To despise such a guide is a kind of arrogance; unless of course you know the area better, in which case you are probably writing a long-distance footpath guidebook yourself. This leads neatly to Wainwright.

Though the excellence of the Pennine Way reflects upon its creator, Tom Stephenson, and though his guide (HMSO) as creator will always be the most authoritative, the sheer artistic skill and cartographical magic of A. Wainwright, make his own guide to the Pennine Way, like his Lakeland guides, an invaluable part of every Pennine wayfarer's collection.

Wainwright faces that terrible moral dilemma of all guidebook writers. Your guidebook can be purchased by sinner as well as saint, by the loutish as well as the responsible and well behaved. But at the time of the publication of his *Coast to Coast Walk* in 1972 he was beginning to have second thoughts about long-distance footpaths and the "problems" they seemed to bring.

And yet, whilst he was bemoaning that very fact, his Coast to Coast Walk was creating a new long-distance path, from St Bees Head on the Irish sea coast, in Cumbria, to Robin Hood's Bay – one hundred and ninety miles across England, traversing three National Parks, the Lakes, the Moors and the Yorkshire Dales.

The route through the Dales really is very good. From Kirkby Stephen the "Coast to Coast" as inevitably it is known, climbs through Hartley to the strange, weird cairns on Nine Standards Rigg – a thrilling climb, much loved by northern fell walkers. It then crosses into Swaledale via Raven Seat and Whitsundale to Keld, then across the most spectacular of the lead-mining area from Swinnergill to Gunnerside Gill and Old Gang, before descending to Reeth, downriver to Marrick Priory, Marrick, Marske and along Whitecliffe to Richmond.

The total of forty-five miles from Kirkby Stephen to Richmond makes a lovely and highly satisfying northern crossing of the Dales. The excellence of Wainwright's work will ensure its popularity for many years to come. Already signposts have the initials "CC", a quiet formalization of the personal vision and the unofficial recognition of an artist's and writer's success. Boots follow words – and pictures. Again, there is nothing new in this; some of our old mapmakers then produced the kind of maps that you rolled up to read on horseback twisting the scroll to read the appropriate piece as you galloped on in the rain. Because people followed the mapmaker's chosen route, the road builders came behind, and Wainwright's Coast to Coast will be a clear line on the ground as well as a map for years to come.

Maybe the real answer to the accusation that long-distance paths create "pedestrian motorways" is to take the motorway analogy a little further and, just as Britain did not regard the M1 as the only available route, so other "official" paths – the Cleveland

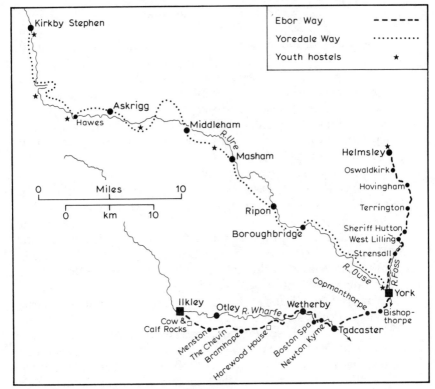

THE EBOR AND YOREDALE WAYS

Way, Offa's Dyke Path, the Cornish Coast Path and so on have come into being through the efforts of the local authorities and the Countryside Commission. Equally, writers and consumers' groups paths, "ramblers' ways" have come into being through the efforts of individuals, rambling clubs, walking groups, the Ramblers' Association, often establishing the route by usage rather than the cumbersome sledgehammer of formal agreements and orders.

A recent example has been Ken Piggin's Yoredale Way. Ken Piggin, who lives in York, had, with the help of colleagues in the Ebor Acorn Walking Club, created an Ebor Way, a seventy-two mile long route from Helmsley to Ilkley via York, thus connecting up the Cleveland Way through the North Moors with the Dales Way through the Dales, a kind of Dales – Moors link. In 1980 he completed work on the Yoredale Way which follows the Rivers Ouse and Ure from York to Kirkby Stephen, making a particularly lovely walk through Wensleydale from Middleham to Aysgarth and Hawes, climbing through Cotterdale and up Cotter End to follow the High Way over Hell Gill and along the River Eden past Pendragon Castle to Kirkby Stephen. It is another fine walk, well served by youth hostels and villages, and for that reason, like all well-planned long-distance paths, certain to bring extra trade and custom to Dales communities. It is known as the Yoredale Way because Yoredale is the old name for Wensleydale and includes the lower part of the river valley.

I have saved the Dales Way, for many and personal reasons, until last. The Dales Way owes its existence to an idea, in the late '60s, of getting a riverside footpath up every river valley in the Dales. This concept was pursued by the West Riding Area of the Ramblers' Association and in particular its then Footpaths Secretary, Tom Wilcock. Told that they should concentrate their efforts on one major path to achieve any result, the ramblers chose the Wharfe Valley. But a path from Ilkley, in the middle of Wharfedale to the source of the river, would merely end in a Pennine bog high on Cam Fell; so why not continue over the watershed to the Dee and Dentdale? From Sedbergh it was but a good day's walk into the Lake District so why not follow the Lune, the Mint, the Kent into what was then Westmorland and across to the magic shores of Windermere.

That was how the idea of an eighty-one mile essentially riverside route was born. The name Dales Way was chosen because it not only was essentially a valley and therefore a "dale" route (with the exception, of course, of the ascent of Cam Fell) but it also crossed the entire Dales area from south-east to north-west.

It is, in my truly biased opinion, one of the loveliest walks of all, starting from Ilkley Bridge, with, for the totally dedicated, optional pedestrian links from Leeds and even Bradford, it follows the river to Bolton Abbey, Barden, Burnsall and Grassington; then over the high limestone pavement to Kettlewell. Back along the riverside to Starbotton and Buckden, and along Langstrothdale, with the river threading its way between spring celandines, to Hubberholme, Yockenthwaite, Deepdale, Beckermonds, Oughtershaw, the very names a kind of deep-throated music.

The ascent of Cam is a little out of character – no longer alongside the sound and movement of the river, but across high, thin pastures and moorland. At Cam is one of two experimental "camping barns" to welcome Dales Way walkers; the other is at Cat Holes, south-west of Sedbergh. These are run by the farmer with a grant from the Countryside Commission and consist of simple but comfortable accommodation in a converted barn. Details and information can be obtained from the National Park office. From Cam the Dales Way cuts through the afforestation to join the Pennine Way on the old Roman road, before descending westwards to cross the River Dee and the Hawes road near Gearstones, then a moorland path past High Gayle to Dentdale, then following a combination of quiet lane, field paths and riverside paths down this most intimate and individual of dales to Dent town.

From Dent, riverside and quiet lane face the walker before climbing into the lovely vale dominated by the Howgill Fells and Sedbergh. Again some lovely stretches of riverside are traced along the Rawthey, before the Dales Way twists northwards along the rocky banks of the upper Lune into the Lune Gorge, cutting across the motorway and railway before entering the quite distinctive countryside east of Kendal, the spiky Silurian crags giving an entirely different flavour to the landscape between Burneside and Staveley.

In its last few miles, the Dales Way again leaves the riversides, climbing by lane and moorland path to a most spectacular viewpoint where the walker suddenly peers into the great chasm of Windermere before descending through the straggle of Bowness, to the shores of the lake. But strictly speaking that is beyond the scope of this book.

Quality of landscape is a highly subjective area, the quality of a walk, of any kind, even more so. Suffice it to say that many long-distance footpath walkers, the kind who enjoy their paths and do not see them as things to be "bagged" at the greatest possible speed, have told me that the Dales Way is their favourite or is among their favourite routes. And many have not only said they want to do it again, but actually do repeat the experience. You might well meet some of them at it.

Riverside paths have a lot to offer, and it would make sense to have other riverside routes, climbing up to daleheads, meeting, offering a spider's web of routes through the Dales, with cross-dale routes and inter-dale routes filling the network.

Some people would regard this as a nightmare. But the paths

already exist in most cases. Where they do not, powers, re-sources, and often the goodwill exist to create them. Austria, Switzerland, parts of Germany, have such a density of beautifully waymarked routes. The system offers many choices, many possi-bilities.

I see such a network evolving in the Dales. The older, estab-lished routes will remain as the arteries, with others still to come (the Ribble and the Nidd are obvious candidates), but with the addition of smaller veins and capillaries, secondary routes, link-ing routes, the load will be spread. Many more people will, I suspect, be using footpaths in the future, because that future will, I also suspect, offer more leisure or freedom from work as the microchip revolution occurs. When we have learned to use that leisure positively, then walking footpaths will offer a rewarding and satisfying way of discovering our environment and the rich network of longer routes now evolving is simply restoring a part of a heritage which we thought we had lost.

REFERENCE

The Pennine Way, Tom Stephenson (HMSO, 1979)
Pennine Way Companion, A. Wainwright (Westmorland Gazette, 1968)
The Pennine Way, Kenneth Oldham (Dalesman, 1970)
A Coast to Coast Walk, A. Wainwright (Westmorland Gazette, 1973)
The Ebor Way, Ken Piggin (Dalesman, 1978)
The Yoredale Way, Ken Piggin (Dalesman, 1980)
The Dales Way, Colin Speakman (Dalesman, 1970)
A Dales Way Map, Colin Speakman and Arthur Gemmell (Stile Publications, 1982)
Ramblers' Way, David Sharp (ed) (David & Charles, 1980)

14

The Dales Rail Story

The Settle–Carlisle line is the most splendid railway line in all England. It was built late in the railway building era, in the 1870s, as a result of bitter economic warfare between two of the largest railway companies, the London and North Western and the mighty Midland Railway. The source of the conflict was traffic to Scotland, the Midland Railway having to use LNWR lines from Ingleton to Carlisle, and the LNWR doing everything possible to delay, inconvenience or hinder Midland traffic in favour of their own crack expresses over the Shap route.

The solution, a daring one, was to build a line not simply across the Pennines – that had been done several times before – but along them, from Ribblesdale to the Eden Valley, across or through the highest watersheds.

The proposal frightened even the Midland, both in terms of the engineering problems the line posed and the cost of that engineering. When in 1868 the Bill to build the line was finally presented to Parliament, the LNWR, realizing the Midland were serious, offered much more favourable and reasonable terms. The Midland hastily tried to withdraw the Bill. But Parliament, tired of railway speculators wasting their time with abortive schemes, decided the line had to go ahead, as it were *"pour encourager les autres"*.

The story of the actual building of that line is one of the great heroic tales of railway literature, requiring as it did an army of Irish navvies, living and working in the wild and windy Pennines for seven years until the line was finally completed in 1876.

The Settle–Carlisle was indeed a line built on a heroic scale, a main line where a mountain railway should run, with huge viaducts and tunnels to cross the valleys and penetrate the fells, designed to carry the Midland's principal Anglo-Scottish traffic.

The line is still the largest man-made structure in the Dales, a structure comparable in the scale of its construction with the pyramids of the Nile. With the line came a characteristic railway architecture to the Dales – the Derby Gothic – its stations, signal-boxes, railway cottages, warehouses, bringing a new way of life and economic growth to the area, particularly the dairy industry of Upper Wharfedale (a branch of the line was opened to Hawes) and the Eden Valley.

When the railways lost their monopoly after the First World War, and the dramatic growth of private cars, lorries and coaches in the 1950s and 1960s made enormous inroads into the profitability of railways, the Settle–Carlisle line with its huge maintenance costs, was an early target of the Beeching rationalization programme. It was expected to be closed by 1970.

Thankfully, nothing of the kind had yet happened. This is entirely due to the effect of electrifying the West Coast Main Line over Shap – ironically the rival LNWR route that caused the line to be built in the first place. High-speed trains created line capacity problems and the old Midland line had to carry slow freight. It was also vital to have a relief line available to allow maintenance and engineering works on the electrified line, so the Settle–Carlisle line, for strategic reasons, must be available for the foreseeable future to allow British Rail to operate services to compete with the airlines. Improved Nottingham–Leeds–Glasgow trains have replaced the old Thames–Clyde expresses retaining an important direct passenger link between the East Midlands, Yorkshire and Scotland.

But strategic reasons could do nothing for local services on the line. Since the 1870s stations such as Horton in Ribblesdale, Ribblehead, Dent and Garsdale as well as providing for the needs of local communities have provided a marvellous means of access for ramblers from the old West Riding travelling to the Yorkshire Dales. Indeed many of the early guidebooks to that part of the Dales were written around the line, and suggested attractions which you could reach from particular stations.

I well recall, as a student and then as a young schoolmaster in West Riding, spending many a weekend travelling to the Dales behind a grimy "Black Five" locomotive, all steam and iron, hauling its two or three coaches from Hellifield "all stations to Carlisle", giving you, providing you planned your time carefully,

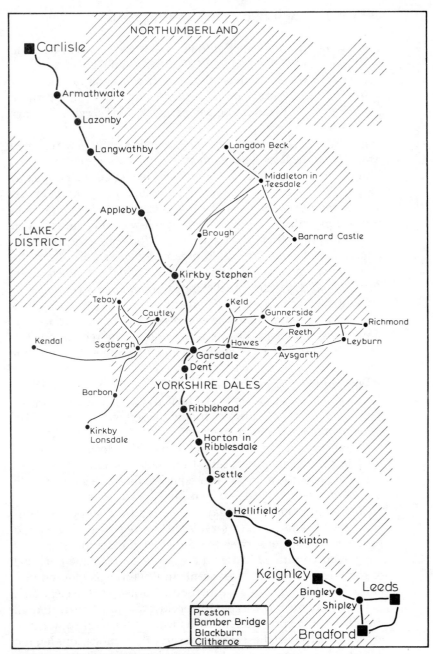

DALES RAIL NETWORK – 1981

a full long afternoon in Dentdale, Whernside, Wild Boar Fell, with time, I recall, to get right up to Kirkby Stephen if you kept an eye on your watch. Without the train there was simply no other way of getting there – buses if they could run at all on those narrow roads only ran the occasional market day service of no use to walkers.

But the local stations also carried excursion traffic. Two or three times a year the Ramblers' Association, West Riding Area, would bring all their members and the many federated walking clubs together to travel on an excursion train, and the favourite excursion of the year was along the Settle–Carlisle line, by common consent providing access to the best fell-walking country in all Yorkshire, and that, if you lived in Yorkshire, meant in all England. The ramblers would organize guided walks from the trains, a complex programme labelled "easy", "moderate" or "strenuous" depending on distance and terrain, with each leader carrying the appropriate coloured armband. Many walking clubs also used the service and the excursions were quite social occasions, with old colleagues from throughout the region meeting on the trains. There were also regular excursions from Manchester.

But Beeching threatened all that. The steely-eyed economists from Whitehall, mistakenly as it turned out, had no brief for the sentimental value of railways, for the convenience of a handful of local people living high in the Pennines or for the needs of ramblers. Local services were put forward for closure as early as 1964 but the Transport Users' Consultative Committee firmly declared, after the appropriate enquiries, that the closure would cause "very severe hardship" if it went ahead.

The government of the day agreed, and the stopping trains were saved. Diesel railcars replaced the old steam trains and paytrain guards took over the duties of the station staff. But passengers continued to dwindle away, and the tourist potential of the line, one of the most scenic in Britain, was ignored. So, hardly had the cheering of the Settle-Carlisle enthusiasts died down, before the line was put up for closure again, and despite all the efforts of the protesters, which included the local authorities, in May 1970 the last diesel railcar to serve the local stations left the deserted platforms and that, it seemed, was that. A few people commented bitterly that a National Park had been created in the

Dales which people were no longer able to reach unless they were fortunate enough to own a car.

There could not even be the occasional excursion train because at that time British Rail, deeply concerned with its Inter-City image, was not concerned about such marginal trade and, in any case, was not too keen to allow trains to call again at closed stations. The situation was hopeless. Some of us bought cars, others resigned ourselves to favourite walks nearer at home.

From the merest acorns we are told mightiest oaks flourish. The particular acorn that started the Dales Rail fever began one cold, wet Easter Monday on a ramble in the South Pennines when, having lunch in the lea of a wall, the more nostalgic members of the group began to berate the folly of the men who ran the railways. It appeared mere logic that a train running up "the Long Drag" would be packed to the roof with ramblers. "So why not charter a train from BR and prove it?" said someone. The acorn had landed on soft earth. In July that year, 1974, after heated arguments amongst the ramblers themselves whether to put such money at risk, the train ran, calling at Garsdale and Kirkby Stephen Stations, to Appleby.

It was a triumph. As well as over five hundred walkers filling a ten-coach train to the luggage racks, local people stood on Garsdale Station platform, their eyes heavy with nostalgia, to see the old station back in life again.

And a fact relevant to all Yorkshiremen, the train had made a profit. The Ramblers' Association were delighted.

But by the autumn of 1974 the dead hand of officialdom had struck again. It would appear vitally necessary to demolish the disused platforms on the Settle–Carlisle line to ensure sufficient clearance for the new longer Mark III coaches that would be using the line when relief trains ran.

And to rub salt into the wound, at Ribblehead Station, a vital departure point for many a splendid walk to Whernside and the Three Peaks area, the entire platform and waiting-room were demolished on the "down" platform to make way for a new quarry railhead siding. The dastardly deed was done so quickly that Mr Roland Eames who was living at Ribblehead Station House at the time and who tenanted the waiting-room where he stored some scientific equipment, woke one morning and watched from his bedroom window in alarm as a bulldozer reared towards the waiting-room and his equipment.

Enter, at this critical moment, from stage right, a Fairy God-mother in the form of the newly reconstituted Yorkshire Dales National Park Committee who immediately made contact with British Rail. A formula was worked out to provide a degree of financial support to keep the station platforms available for future use.

There was little point in safeguarding empty railway-station platforms if trains were not to use them. And so from this point developed an almost unparalleled special partnership between British Rail and the Yorkshire Dales National Park Committee, under its able chairman at that time, Keith Lockyer, of Grassington. It was Keith Lockyer, more than anyone else, who provided the political will to get the scheme off the ground. The initiative was soon to receive support from other major local authorities and the Countryside Commission in the region.

The initial idea was a simple one. To charter a train as the ramblers had done, from Leeds to Appleby, but also to offer a service for the local community by running the same train, after it had emptied out the hikers and the visitors, back to Leeds or Bradford for shopping purposes.

It was an elegant concept. The local community had suffered, after all, the loss of a vital lifeline when the line closed. Their needs were every bit as important – many people would argue more important – than those of the city dwellers denied access to their open countryside. By running the train back, costs were kept to a minimum and, if you could fill the trains both ways, you could cover costs quite easily.

But there was more to achieve. Following the Swiss concept of a truly integrated transport service, it was decided to operate connecting bus services from the nearby towns of Hawes and Sedbergh to Garsdale Station, giving local people access to the train, and allowing visitors to reach the magnificent country around the Howgill Fells and Upper Wensleydale.

It was agreed to run this double service on Saturdays, but on Sundays to run simply to Appleby without the return trip as shopping services were not required. The buses were extended to Swaledale and to Cautley Spout to increase recreational opportunities.

As a pilot, the committee agreed to support the operation over three weekends in the spring of 1975. Ticket prices were to be kept to an absolute minimum to cover costs, a simple brand name "Dales Rail" was conceived to give the service an identity, and a simple leaflet produced and distributed to potential passengers.

Last-minute hitches over safety regulations at stations delayed publicity to only a few days before and as the final few days slipped away before the launching of the service, and few bookings were received, the awful doubt remained if in fact, five years after the railway had closed, anyone would still want to use it.

In the event, on a lovely May Saturday, the train was well filled, albeit with officials and local dignitaries trying out the new service. Quite a few walkers came on the Sunday too, attracted by an ambitious programme of guided walks laid on by the National Park's voluntary warden service.

If May was promising, June was an outright success, with the train in both directions almost fully booked.

And if June was a success, July was a triumph, with huge numbers not only of walkers but of local people turning out to try out their new service. Extra carriages were ordered from British Rail, but even this was insufficient to cope with the one hundred and ninety-nine people who crowded Kirkby Stephen station platform. It was standing-room only on the train and the National Park Committee had achieved the inconceivable – made a substantial profit on running a train service.

Clearly, Dales Rail now had a future. Support came from many sources, including other local authorities along the line, Cumbria County Council and Eden District Council, but above all from the Countryside Commission who, recognizing the national implications of reopening a railway through a National Park, were prepared to consider Dales Rail as an experiment, and to appoint a Project Officer, Andrew McCullough, to steer the scheme through its experimental phase.

With this kind of support, the committee developed the experiment in the later part of the glorious summer of 1975, operating a Friday service from Carlisle which returned on Friday evening with weekenders for the Dales, and a service from East Lancashire over the freight-only Blackburn–Hellifield line. The results provided valuable experience on which to base the 1976 season.

An early development was to look at more stations in the Eden

Valley district of Cumbria–Langwathby, Lazonby and Armath-
waite were selected – and with support from the commission and
Cumbria County Council to reopen these for an improved Saturday service which now ran direct to Carlisle, with a second train
operating direct from Carlisle to Leeds. Interest in the service
continued to grow. People used it for shopping, sightseeing and
visiting friends and relations. Whole families, separated for
years, were united. An octogenarian lady living in Garsdale was
able to see her brother in Kirkby Stephen, for the first time in two
years by using the train. An elderly lady from Bradford who
hitherto could only visit a relative in Dent by means of an
occasional, expensive taxi ride, could now travel two or three
times a year by Dales Rail to Dent Station. A young couple were
able to visit their parents in Hawes. But above all, it was the
walkers who brought the service to life, some of them the older
generation who had used the train in former years and were
delighted to have their access to the hills restored, many of them
younger people, without cars, who were able to discover for the
first time the glories of that part of the countryside and the value
of getting there by a fast and inexpensive public transport service.
Walking clubs used the service, so did individuals. Up to a
thousand people might use the service on a busy weekend, and
some would come several times a year. Youth hostellers would
travel up on Saturday morning and stay at some remote Pennine
hostel before returning on Sunday evening. Cyclists could take
their bikes initially for a small charge and later, in line with BR
practice, free of charge.

Dales Rail trains have a unique atmosphere, difficult to define
exactly. A *Guardian* journalist described Dales Rail as a "carnival
train" perhaps because of the bright red stickers identifying the
Dales Rail specials; but more because of the convivial, enthusiastic atmosphere generated among passengers and voluntary staff.
It was, in a real sense, *their* service, offering a uniquely beautiful
journey, splendid walks, and a degree of service typified by the
fact that when you arrived at the railhead the buses were waiting
for you even if the train was late, the guide for the guided walk
was waiting for you on the platform, someone would sell you a
leaflet, or a booklet or a cup of tea on the train. On Dales Rail,
people cared.

A key to the whole concept has been the voluntary element. By agreement with British Rail, and because it was a "charter" service, voluntary stewards, mainly rail or public transport enthusiasts with a deep love and interest in the line, were able to assist passengers, ensure that everything was in order, make the passenger feel part of something worthwhile. British Rail staff, at all levels, responded to the challenge, co-operated fully with the spirit of the occasion and were genuinely delighted to see well-filled trains. The bus drivers too, on the linking National Bus Company Services at Garsdale, did much to ensure the smooth running of the service, that connections were met and passengers, whether visitors or local people, got home safely.

Between 1976 and 1980 the service expanded carefully. A regular service from Lancashire was added, with trains from Preston and Blackburn coupling up at Hellifield with trains from Leeds on Saturdays. Thanks to the efforts of Ribble Valley District Council, Clitheroe Station, another early victim of the Beeching axe despite the fact that it served a community of 12,000, was reopened and, with the local band playing, the first train left Clitheroe for the Yorkshire Dales and Carlisle early in 1977. A Christmas shoppers' service was instigated for the benefit of local people in December, and proved a huge success, with the inevitable Father Christmas introduced for the sake of children and doubtless their accompanying parents. Walkers from Carlisle also used the December train, having a day's winter walking in the fells on the same service.

It was realized that, by the late '70s, the Carlisle–Leeds service, serving very small communities, could not justify a monthly service unless costs were to escalate. So it was decided to run the service over the Clitheroe line to Blackpool, still providing connections with the Inter-City train at Settle, but giving people a huge choice of shopping and now seaside trips. Another innovation was the use of the truncated Wensleydale railway line between Northallerton and Redmire. This branch, which once ran right through Wensleydale to connect with the Midland's Settle–Carlisle line at Hawes, remains open for limestone trains for Teeside from the quarries above Redmire. As serviceable stations still exist passenger trains can, on an occasional basis, travel to and from Redmire, Leyburn and Bedale.

Twice a year, therefore, trains now operate from West Yorkshire (and on one occasion Tyneside) to Northallerton before travelling along the branch. At Redmire connecting buses meet the trains from villages in Upper Wensleydale and Swaledale, and collect passengers from the train. The train then runs back to York, to give Dalesfolk a full afternoon out amid the shops and sights of one of England's most famous cities. As on the Settle–Carlisle line, this service is only possible because the ramblers from the cities in effect cross-subsidize the operation, thus proving with Dales transport, as for many other matters, the interests of townsfolk and countryfolk need not be seen to be mutually incompatible.

After the ending of the experimental phase, it was realized that the sheer complexity of the service was beyond the means of the National Park Committee to cope with. An important development from 1979 was the involvement of West Yorkshire Passenger Transport Executive who were immediately able to bring their marketing resources into operation, providing as Dales Rail did an important recreational service for people from West Yorkshire. This increased and improved the financial viability of the service. The Lancashire and Carlisle services were now operated as "guaranteed" excursions by British Rail, with the support being provided by a unique consortium of authorities, including the Park Committee, Cumbria and Lancashire County Councils and by the Countryside Commission.

This level of co-operation between British Rail, the National Bus Company and a number of participating authorities is something quite unique in the British Isles. A steering group of officers meets regularly to approve, in the light of available resources, the programme for the year, and to solve all the many problems of ticketing, line availability, bus connections and the like to make a truly integrated and comprehensive recreational service work.

For Dales Rail is not just a transport service; it is a recreational service offering participants insight and understanding of the countryside. The guided walks are led by men and women of real and deep knowledge of the Dales and the Eden Valley, who are able to interpret the countryside and to communicate something of their own involvement and respect for the environment, and the attitude of mind that goes with it. At the end of the day it is an educational service, a system of ideas about rural transport, about the environment, which have implied values. It is more than merely learning a few basic rules – about fell craft, about not climbing walls, not trampling meadowland. It is something which is caught rather than taught and suggests the kind of idealism which the founding fathers of the National Park movement in England and Wales fully understood and appreciated.

What of the future of Dales Rail in the bleak '80s? We live in a profoundly uncertain age, where events in the Middle East or Asia have a profounder effect on our lives than anything we can achieve. Dales Rail, for all its self-evident success, needs scarce public money if it is to survive, for the simple reason that if people of average or limited means are to use it, fares must be kept low and with rising costs, even well-filled trains barely cover their operational costs let alone such extras as marketing, publicity and administration. If the modest trickle of support for Dales Rail is turned off, then the service will cease.

But the most serious threat of all, at time of writing, is British Rail's proposal to close the entire Settle–Carlisle line. Few people dispute the view that up to £20 million will be required over the next two decades to repair or even rebuild Ribblehead, Arten Gill and Denthead viaducts and to tackle a huge backlog of other essential work on this great railway, which has suffered the effects of a century's Pennine storms and frosts. More than 20,000 objections to the closure have been received by the Transport Users' Committees from throughout the United Kingdom and even from overseas, many of them from users of Dales Rail, and the closure is likely to be fiercely contested. A strong body of opinion now suggests that the Settle–Carlisle line should be developed as a heritage and recreational facility of national importance.

The outcome is at least as likely to be determined by political as economic considerations.

The real success of Dales Rail has been the goodwill and enthusiasm of the participants, whether train crews, bus drivers, voluntary stewards and walk leaders and passengers. Goodwill and enthusiasm are rare and powerful qualities, even in an age of fashionable despair. Politicians, after all, will only survive themselves if they serve the people, and political will, transplanted into action, can always provide the financial resources. It is up to the users of Dales Rail to ensure that this is so. A significant development is the creation of a flourishing Friends of Dales Rail organization, consisting of voluntary workers and regular passengers, who are likely to help create exactly the kind of support which is needed to see Dales Rail continue, and, in the future, expand.

Taking a wider view, and in the perspective of history, Dales Rail is but a modest little project, carrying a few hundred people from and to the Dales on a fine but neglected railway line on each of a few weekends a year. But it also, in its modest way, represents a victory for the ordinary person, for the consumer, against the blind dictates of economic forces. To a degree its success depended on a tradition, the crowded trains from the old West Riding into the Dales countryside, a folk memory of railways and rambling that still survives, and which, through Dales Rail, has been given a new impetus, with thousands of lives being enriched by the experience. It only happened because enough people cared sufficiently to exert influence, to shape the course of events rather than be shaped by them.

Maybe it is a small but significant symbol of what can be achieved in the Dales as elsewhere, given goodwill, determination and a modicum of good luck. Economics is, in the final analysis, man's servant and not man's master. Perhaps the future of the Dales depends on enough people, outside as well as within the area, sharing a common wish that those rare and precious qualities of the area will, come what may, survive.

REFERENCE

The Midland Railway, F. S. Williams (Strahan and Co., 1877)

The Settle–Carlisle Line, David Joy and W. R. Mitchell (Dalesman, 1966)

The Story of the Settle–Carlisle Line, Frederick W. Houghton and W. Hubert Foster (Huddersfield Advertiser Press, 1948)

Rails in the Fells, David Jenkinson (Peco, 1977)

Dales Rail Guidebook, Yorkshire Dales National Park Committee (YDNP, 1976)

Dales Rail, A report of an experimental project in the Yorkshire Dales National Park–Countryside Commission CCP 120 (HMSO, 1976)

The Settle and Carlisle Railway – a summary report prepared for local authorities (PEIDA, Edinburgh, 1984)

Afterthought

It is always a matter of regret to a topographer, on however modest a scale he operates, that the complex, changing world never remains still long enough for him to get it down on paper. You write about it and, a day later, it is gone, changed, vanished.

Apologies for the transience of all things. Maybe this is why this book cannot be a field guide – field guides must be more precise, require updating more frequently. So bear with me – things were described as I knew them.

On the other hand very many things have hardly changed in a century. If, in another century, this book, with a brown patina of age, should survive on someone's dusty bookshelf, what other changes and similarities will a reader note then? Perhaps our obsession with getting out into the hills and walking footpaths will seem strange, as indeed it did two centuries ago if not one. Perhaps then we shall be a totally urban community, living in cell-like, air-conditioned, temperature-controlled, totally enclosed cities, isolated from the free, wild elements. Or maybe our descendants will be living in a de-industrialized Britain, in rural, self-sufficient communes, using footpaths and pack-horseways as essential means of communication, regarding our habit of walking paths for fun as both curious and decadent. Maybe in such times ramblers will be seen as strange eccentrics, neo-Wordsworthians who saw meaning in the clouds, significance in the rocks, magic in an ancient field path.

But then society changes and human nature does not. Ignoring such unaccountables as nuclear holocausts, it is safe to assume that generations to come are likely to value our heritage at least as highly as we do now. The sense of continuity with the past is part of our present identity; if we allow it to be destroyed we destroy ourselves.

The winding footpath or green pack-horseway of the Dales is as precious, in a different way, as a painting by Turner, Girtin, or Cotman.

And, because men and women are curious, rebellious individualists, creative, they will seek out the old maps, they will search out the old books, they will walk the old footpaths.

Could a writer about the Yorkshire Dales have happier aspirations?

Index